Mrs Hawaii's
N E W   C O O K B O O K

By Laurie Bachran

Kaneohe, Hawaii

This book is lovingly dedicated to my mother who has always been my source of inspiration, and to

My husband Bill, who has never failed to praise my culinary efforts!

Illustrations and cover by Ron Rieman
Design and Typography by Matt and Celia Rawlins
Executive Editing by Ann Rayson and Rebecca Salzer

Preface

The original Mrs. Hawaii's Cookbook was first published in 1964 when the eldest of our six children was ten years old. Now, 25 years later our family includes nine wonderful grandchildren. Realizing the need for a "family style" cookbook with a cosmopolitan flavor and simple yet mouth – watering recipes, I have put together the ones I think are the very best I have ever tried or tasted.

Through the illness of a dear friend, I was made aware of the importance of preventative medicine through proper nutrition and education. I have presented in this revised edition of *Mrs. Hawaii's New Cookbook* a Health Recipe Section that I hope will encourage you to live a new healthy lifestyle.

I would like to thank my friends who gave me their own treasured recipes so that you could also enjoy them.

For the "gourmet touch" I have been privileged to publish the specialties of some of our top island restaurants. These you can try for that extra special dinner.

So mothers, instead of lamenting, "What shall I cook today?" lets say, "E hele mai ai!" or "Come let's eat!"

Laurie Bachran

Table of Contents

Pupus

Coolers

Soups

Salads

Seafood

Entrees

Side Orders

Breads

Desserts

Recipes for Health
Table of Contents

Pupus

Soups

Salads

Entrees

Side Orders

Breads

Desserts

Pupus

Lacy Shrimp Tempura

I like to vary this Shrimp Tempura by serving it with different sauces. One is the usual Hot Mustard and Shoyu Sauce, another, a Chinese Hot sauce or a Pineapple Sauce.

Prepare the shrimp in the following manner.

Remove the shells leaving the tail attached to the shrimp. Remove the black vein from the shrimp's back. Run a sharp knife down the back without quite cutting through. Spread shrimp flat. Flatten shrimp with the dies of a wide blade knife.

Mix	**1/2 cup bisquick**
	1/2 cup cornstarch
	1 egg slightly beaten
Add	**3/4 cup ice water** or enough to make a medium thick batter
Dip	shrimp in batter, holding on to the tail.
Lay	gently in 4 inches hot oil in deep fryer. Turn Once.
Test	oil in the following manner:
	Batter will sink if the oil is too cold. Batter will disperse if the oil is too hot. Batter will sink then rise when the oil is just right.

Chinese Hot Sauce

Blend
1/2 cup cider vinegar
1/2 cup water
1/2 cup sugar
1 Tablespoon cornstarch
3-4 dashes red liquid Chinese pepper or Tobasco
(more or less to taste) shoyu to color light brown

Cook
on medium heat until sauce thickens slightly

Pineapple Sauce

Mix
4 Tablespoons sugar
2 Tablespoons cornstarch
4 Tablespoons pineapple juice
4 Tablespoons white vinegar in saucepan
until sauce thickens (5 Minutes)

Garnish
with pineapple chunks and Chinese parsley

Hot Mustard Sauce

Mix Coleman's dry mustard according to the directions. Use about **1 teaspoon of mixed mustard in 1/2 cup of shoyu.** Add more mustard for a hotter taste.

Shrimp Puffs

These are especially good as pupus or as a side dish with your Chinese dinner. Serve with Pineapple Sauce, Mustard and Shoyu Sauce or Chinese Hot Sauce.

Shell
1 lb. fresh shrimp. Clean and chop fine

Add
8-10 water chestnuts, chopped fine
1 Tablespoon cornstarch
1 teaspoon sweet white wine

14

1/2 teaspoon salt
1 egg, slightly beaten

Mix   well and shape into dollar size round balls.

Fry   in deep oil until golden brown. Drain on absorbent paper.

Rumaki

Halve   **10 water chestnuts**

Quarter   **5 chicken livers**

Cut   **10 slices bacon** in half

Take   one piece of water chestnut, one piece of chicken liver and wrap in 1/2 slice of bacon. Secure with toothpick

Marinate   rumakis in
1 Tablespoon white wine
1/4 cup shoyu
2 Tablespoons brown sugar
1/2 teaspoon grated ginger root
Refrigerate rumakis in marinade for 2 hours

Broil   over charcoal or under broiler. Baste and turn until bacon is crisp.

Dippy Shrimp-Ono Ono

Blend   **1/2 lb. cooked shrimp,** chopped fine
1 cup creamed cottage cheese
1 cup sour cream
2 Tablespoons A.1. sauce
2 Tablespoons lemon juice
2 Tablespoons chili sauce
1 teaspoon salt
Dash of fresh ground pepper

Mix   well. Serve with chips. (3 cups)

*ono, ono-very good

Pickled Cucumbers

Mrs. Clem Akina graciously gave me this recipe. Try it. It's terrific!

Wash	and slice **8-10 cucumbers** Put into large pan
Sprinkle	with **salt** and soak 3 hours in lots of ice cubes
Heat	**3 1/2 cups cider vinegar** **3 1/2 cups sugar** **1 teaspoon salt** **1 1/2 teaspoon tumeric** **1 1/2 teaspoon mustard seeds** **1 1/2 teaspoon celery seeds** Do not boil mixture
Add	drained cucumbers and stir Remove and bottle in sterile jars

Won Ton

Buy	**1 box of won ton pi or squares**
Combine	**3/4 lb. fresh ground pork** **1/2 lb. finely chopped shrimp** **10 water chestnuts,** finely chopped **6 stalks of green onions,** finely chopped **1 teaspoon salt** **1 Tablespoon shoyu** **Dash of white pepper** **1 Tablespoon sweet wine.** Mix well.
Place	1/2 teaspoon of pork mixture in the center of the won ton square. Brush the edges with water. Fold in half and twist the corners.
Fry	in deep fat until golden brown.
Serve	plain or with Hot Mustard and Shoyu Sauce.

16

Gau Gee

Use	the same recipe as above only
Put	**1 slightly rounded teaspoon** of filling in each square
Fold	in half, sealing edges with water

*Both Won Ton and Gau Gee may be cooked in a deep pot of boiling water and served in soup. Boil Won Ton for 3-5 minutes and Gau Gee from 5-8 minutes. Drain, serve in a chicken broth with boiled saimin or boiled Poppy Brand Chinese Mein noodles. Serve with hot Mustard and Shoyu sauce for dipping. Garnish with Chinese parsley and Ham strips.

Bar-B-Que Sticks

Marinate	**1 lb. sirloin tip**, tenderloin or flank steak, cut in thin strips in **3/4 cup shoyu** **1/2 cup sugar** **1/2 inch ginger root**, crushed **1 oz. sweet white wine for 1-2 hours**
Skewer	meat on sticks threading meat in and out using 2-3 pieces of meat to a stick.
Bra-B-Que	over charcoal a few minutes on each side.

*Make Kabobs by alternating meat with whole button mushrooms and pineapple chunks. Baste with marinade.

Teriyaki Meatballs

Doris Hironaka, who excels in Japanese cooking, has passed on one of her favorite party pupus.

Mix	**1/2 cup shoyu** **1/2 cup water** **1 Tablespoon Worcestershire** **2 small cloves garlic**, pressed **1 teaspoon ginger juice** (freshly pressed) **3 lbs. Ground chuck** **1 Tablespoon parsley** **12-15 minced water chestnuts** and roll into balls
Place	on a cookie sheet lined with foil
Bake	at 275 degrees oven for 15 – 20 minutes

Pizzalanis

Second place winner in Junior Miss Contest 1970! A teenage favorite.

Bake	**8 oz. sharp cheddar cheese**, grated **1/8 teaspoon powdered oregano** **1/4 teaspoon onion salt** **1/4 teaspoon garlic salt** **With enough mayonnaise** to moisten
Spread	on **4 English muffin halves**
Place	under broiler for a few minutes to melt cheese mixture
Add	**8 slices peeled tomatoes**
Top	with **12 slices Portuguese sausage or pepperoni**
Place	under broiler until sausage is browned
Top	with **8 pitted black olives** fastening with toothpick
Decorate	with Vanda Orchid

Mango Chutney Pupu

A fiery pupu to accompany your favorite cooler.

Mix	**1 cup grated cheddar cheese** **1 cup chopped mango chutney** **4-6 dashes Tabasco sauce**
Put	**1 teaspoon of mixture on a Ritz cracker**
Bake	till bubbly at 350 degree oven. Serve immediately!
Serves	8 people.

Hawaiian Fruit Salad

Halve	**2 firm ripe papayas** and scoop out seeds
Scoop	out fruit carefully leaving1/4 inch rim
Cut	fruit into sections and place back in shell
Add	**4 ripe bananas,** cut in sections **4 slices of fresh pineapple** cut into sections or pineapple chunks
Squeeze	**juice of 1 lime over fruit and fold in** **2 sprigs of freshly chopped mint**

Chill and serve

Pineapple Surprise

Cut	off top of **1 whole pineapple**
Cut off	1/2 inch slice at base of pineapple
Insert	knife 1/2 inch in from the pineapple skin and cut in a complete circle from top to bottom
Lift	out fruit and cut into cubes, first removing the center core
Sweeten	fruit with ¼ **cup sugar**, more or less to taste **1 oz. light rum**
Place	shell on serving dish. Put fruit back into the pineapple shell and cover it with pineapple top. This will make a lovely centerpiece for your Hawaiian table setting.

Sashimi

Bone	**1 lb. fresh Ahi or Swordfish** and chill
Slice	very thin
Arrange	on a bed of **shredded lettuce** and serve with **Hot Mustard and Shoyu Sauce.**

Coolers

Mai Tai

From Trader Vic's comes the exotic Mai Tai, as only they prepare it. With it comes the warning that only the brave dare drink more than two!

Into   a **14 oz. tub of chipped ice**, add
1 dash of Orange Curacao
1 dash of Orgeat syrup
2 jiggers of unsweetened lemon juice (bottled)
1 jigger of *simple syrup
1 jigger of light rum
1 jigger dark Jamaica rum. Do not stir.

Garnish   with **sprig of fresh mint**
1 Vanda Orchid (optional)
Sugar cane stick for stirring

***Simple syrup may be purchased in the stores or you can make it yourself by bringing to boil – 1/2 cup sugar with 1 cup of water. Cool and bottle.**

Meyer's Christmas "Goody"

A mellow blend of "Christmas Spirits" from Harry and Emma Meyers kama'aina household. Prepare this recipe one month before Christmas.

Squeeze	5 lbs. oranges, put juice and pulp into a large pot
Add	**8 ozs. Lemon juice** (bottle) **8 ozs. Water** **7 bunches fresh mint,** cut ends off **1 cup brown sugar** **4 cups white sugar** Bring contents to a boil and simmer until mint leaves turn brown. Cool, pour contents into a gallon jar.
Add	**1 qt. bourbon,** keep refrigerated for one month Strain before serving
Pour	mixture over chipped ice, about halfway into an old-fashioned glass
Add	**1 jigger of bourbon**
Fill	the rest of the glass with **ginger ale** Top with a sprig of fresh mint

Duke's Pearl

Nadine and Duke Kahanamoku graciously gave me the recipe for one of their exotic drinks. Served at the former Duke's at Waikiki.

Into	a 7 oz. glass
Add	**3/4 oz. light rum** **3/4 oz. dark rum** **1/2 oz. honey**
Fill	the glass with **passion fruit juice** **juice from a quarter section of lime,** and **chipped ice**
Pour	the contents in a blender for a fast whirl Pour, add your pearl and serve

Molokai Mule

An instant refresher with a kick.

Whirl
in a blender
1 large scoop guava or passion fruit sherbet
1 jigger white Bacardi rum
Serve in frosted sherbet glasses

Silver Fizz

Fill
blender 1/2 full of ice

Add
juice of 1 lime or lemon
1 1/2 teaspoon white sugar
1 jigger vodka
2 egg whites
2 jigger's milk or light cream

Blend
on high speed until ice is crushed
Serve in sherbet glasses with a short straw

Waikiki Chi Chi

Mix
into blender
2 oz. pineapple juice
2 oz. lemon juice
1 oz. coconut syrup
2 oz. vodka
Blend well

Pour
over crushed ice, decorate with mint sprig or cherry

Poi Cocktail

Blend
2 Tablespoons of fresh poi
1 rounded Tablespoon sugar
1 teaspoon rum
1 cup cold milk in a blender

Serve
immediately, in tall, frosted glass

Oahu Country Club Iced Tea

Brew	**tea** to taste
Dip	**mint leaves** in tea for 5 minutes
Add	to each 14 oz. glass **Juice to 1/2 lemon** **1 Tablespoon pineapple juice** **3 teaspoons sugar**
Place	in cocktail shaker and shake well
Serve	over ice. Add a spear of **fresh pineapple**

Sangria Wine Punch

Horace Sutton, well-traveled editor of the *Paradise of the Pacific* magazine and Travel Editor of the *Saturday Review of Literature*, shares one of his recipes acquired in Spain. A definite refresher!

Add	juice and curled peelings of **3 oranges** **2 lemons to** **1/2 gallon burgundy**
Chill	overnight
Add	**1 qt. plain soda water** before serving
Serve	over ice, adding some of the peelings in each glass

***Sautérne may be used with fresh sliced peaches.
Chill overnight. Add soda before serving.**

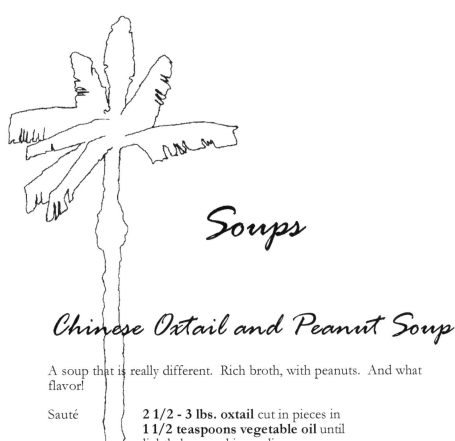

Soups

Chinese Oxtail and Peanut Soup

A soup that is really different. Rich broth, with peanuts. And what flavor!

Sauté	**2 1/2 - 3 lbs. oxtail** cut in pieces in **1 1/2 teaspoons vegetable oil** until lightly browned in medium saucepan
Add	**3/4 teaspoon rock salt**
Mix	**1 inch ginger root, crushed** **1/4 cup sweet white wine** **1/4 cup shoyu together and add to oxtails**
Cover	and cook 3-4 minutes
Add	**1 cup (8oz. package) raw shelled peanuts** **3 cups boiled water**
Simmer	2 1/2 - 3 hours or until oxtails are tender. Skim off fat If soup is too concentrated, add more water.

Yokohama Soup

Chef Louis Chuckey of the Captain's Galley, in one stroke of genius created this superb soup. This is absolutely a must!

Melt	**2 Tablespoons butter**
Add	**2 Tablespoons * shallots,** chopped fine Cook for a few minutes over low heat
Add	**1 Tablespoon flour** and stir for 5 minutes
Add	**2 cups fish stock** **2 cups clam juice** **1 teaspoon cooked spinach,** chopped fine **1/2 cup white wine** **Salt and pepper** to taste
Bring	to a boil and correct seasoning
Whip	**1 cup unsweetened whipped cream**
Pour	soup into individual cups
Top	with whipped cream
Glaze	for 2 minutes under the broiler
Serves	4-6 persons
	*Shallots – the white part of the green onions may be used.

Chicken Wine Soup

A wonderful "pick me up" type of soup for tired mothers.

Sauté	**1 inch sliced root ginger** in **1 Tablespoon oil or chicken fat** until transparent
Add	**1 fresh large fryer** cut in 2 inch pieces Brown lightly
Mix	**3 Tablespoons shoyu** with **3 Tablespoons sweet white wine** or **whiskey**
Pour	over chicken and cover tightly for a few seconds
Add	**2 cups boiled water** and **1/2 teaspoon salt**
Simmer	25-30 minutes or until chicken is tender

Mock Bird's Nest Soup

This makes a wonderful soup. Serve it as a first course to your Chinese dinner.

Soak	**1 roll of Chinese long rice** in water for 1 hour
Make	**a soup stock of chicken bones, necks, wing tips, a ham bone** if you have it
Add	**canned chicken broth,** if necessary to make 3 – 4 cups
Chop	the long rice very fine
Add	to soup stock and simmer until it thickens, about 1/2 hour
Garnish	**with ham and chicken strips and chopped Chinese parsley**
Serve	in bowls with a little shoyu sauce

Salads

Kimi's Lotus and Ginger Root

Pare	**1 section lotus root**
Slice	lotus root into thin rounds and place in bowl
Pour	boiling water, enough to cover and Let stand no longer than 3-5 minutes. Drain immediately.
Boil	**1/2 cup water** **1/2 cup cider vinegar** **1/2 cup sugar (**more or less to taste) **Dash of salt** Simmer for a few minutes
Cool	and pour over lotus root
Slice	**1/2 inch piece of ginger root** very fine
Mix	with lotus root and marinate for a few hours in refrigerator Drain and serve

If Japanese rice vinegar is used, use 1 cup full strength with 1/2 cup sugar. Do not boil.

Potato Pineapple Salad

Prepare potato salad your favorite way. I like to add these ingredients to mine. The secret is to mix the seasonings in while the potatoes are still warm.

Dice	boiled potatoes into small cubes
Add	**to every 3 cups of cubed potatoes** **1 Tablespoon olive oil** **1 Tablespoon vinegar** **1 Tablespoon lemon juice** **1 teaspoon prepared mustard** **1 Tablespoon minced parsley** **3 stalks minced celery** **2 chopped hard boiled eggs** **salt to taste** **freshly ground pepper**
Toss	lightly. Add enough **mayonnaise** to moisten
Add	**1 can chilled, drained pineapple** chunks just before serving. This really does something to potato salad!

Puerto Rican Codfish Salad

Boil	**1 package codfish** for 45 minutes Drain and break into pieces
Cube	**3 large tomatoes**
Slice	**1 round onion**
Add	**2 cloves garlic,** chopped fine or pressed
Pour	**1/4 cup white vinegar,** more or less to taste **1/4 cup salad oil,** more or less to taste
Toss	well and serve. Delicious with poi!

Chinese Chicken Salad

Substantial enough for dinner, this salad may be served warm or chilled.

Thaw	**1 lb. chicken breasts,** and marinate in following sauce for 10-15 minutes **1/4 cup shoyu sauce** **1 clove garlic,** pressed **1 inch ginger root**, sliced or mashed **4 teaspoons sugar** **1/4 teaspoon Chinese Five Spices** **1 Tablespoon white wine**
Deep fry	chicken breasts in hot oil until golden brown Drain and cool on absorbent paper
Slice	**1/4 cup green onions** **1/2 cup celery in julienne**
Wash	**10 lettuce leaves** and tear in small pieces
Cut	**1/4 cup chinese parsley** into 1/2 inch pieces
Shred	chicken breasts and put on large platter or in a deep bowl
Add	**1/8 teaspoon celery salt** **1/8 teaspoon salt** **1/4 teaspoon Chinese Five Spices** Let stand a few minutes
Add	all vegetables to shredded chicken
Sprinkle	**2 teaspoons sesame seeds** **1/2 teaspoon sesame oil** Toss salad well
Add	salt and pepper to taste

Hawaiian Cole Slaw

Crisp and refreshing!

Slice   **1 small head of cabbage (white or red)** very fine
Chop slices into 1/2 inch pieces

Add   **1 small can crushed pineapple**

Add   **3-4 Tablespoons of mayonnaise** to moisten

Chill   in refrigerator until serving time. Serve in little bowls.

Green Goddess Dressing

Combine   **1 quart mayonnaise**
3/4 cup minced chives
3/4 cup chopped parsley
1 Tablespoon tarragon vinegar
1 teaspoon anchovy paste
Salt and pepper to taste and mix well

Refrigerate. Mix well before serving.
Serve on greens-lettuce, chicory, romaine, watercress.

Sour Cream Dressing

Combine   **1 teaspoon salt**
1 teaspoon sugar
1 Tablespoon lemon juice
2 Tablespoons vinegar
Freshly ground pepper
1 cup sour cream

Mix well. Serve on cut assorted fruits

Brandy Sauce

These recipes from the Holiday Award Maile Restaurant at the Kahala Hilton are through the courtesy of the hotel's executive chef, Martin Wyss. The Kahala Hilton is located in Waialae-Kahala, a residential area 10 minutes from Waikiki.

Mix together
2 cups mayonnaise
1 cup ketchup
½ ounce cognac
Few drops lemon juice and **Tabasco sauce**

Fold all ingredients into **1 cup whipped cream.** Mix well.

Delicious over fresh fruit.

Kahala Hilton Celery Seed Dressing

A Kahala Hilton taste treat. Serve over crisp salad greens.

Combine **2 ounces vinegar**
1 teaspoon celery seed
1 teaspoon French mustard
1/6 teaspoon garlic salt or **powder**
1 small egg

Blend in **6 ounces vegetable oil** slowly

Season to taste with
Salt, pepper and Worcestershire sauce

Seafood

Michel's Mahimahi

Chef Sueyoshi of Michel's at the Colony Surf gave a few tips on keeping frozen fish moist. First, you must give the fish a fast thaw in water. Second, soak the fish in milk until it is ready to be cooked. Flour the fish lightly before frying. No more excuses for dry, tasteless fish!

Poach	**4 pieces of fish (6 ozs.) in fish stock or water with mairepox**: i.e., tie in a small piece of net a slice **of onion, parsley, celery, bay leaf**, and immerse in fish stock for 12 -15 minutes
Sauté	**4 Tablespoons chopped onions 3 oz. can of sliced mushrooms** in **2 Tablespoons butter**
Add	**2 ozs. Sautérne**
Add	**3 cups white cream sauce Salt and pepper to taste**
Place	fish on dish and cover with 3/4 of cream sauce
Add	**4 Tablespoons unsweetened whipped cream 2 Tablespoons hollandaise sauce** to remaining cream sauce Stir lightly
Cover	first sauce with second sauce and glaze in 450 degree oven for 1 minute. Serve immediately.

White Cream Sauce

Melt   **6 Tablespoons butter** in top of a double boiler

Blend   **6 Tablespoons pastry flour** to butter until smooth

Add   **3 cups milk**

Cook   until sauce thickens (15 minutes). Stir constantly. Add **salt and pepper** to taste.

Hollandaise Sauce

This sauce may be made and refrigerated. Heat over hot water when ready to serve.

Combine   **3 egg yolks**
                    2 1/2 Tablespoons lemon juice
                    1/4 teaspoon salt
                    Pinch of cayenne
                    Pinch of dry mustard
                    3 Tablespoons vegetable oil
                    Mix well

Cook   over hot water, not boiling, stirring until thick and smooth. If you desire to make the real hollandaise sauce, substitute 1/2 butter for the oil.

Mahimahi Surprise

Light and moist, this will not leave a fishy odor in your kitchen.

Place   **2 lbs. skinned mahimahi pieces** on a broiler rack over a pan

Mix   **2 cups light mayonnaise**
                    2 medium chopped onions

Spread   on mahimahi slices

Sprinkle   with **fresh grated parmesan cheese**

Bake   uncovered at 350 degrees for 45 minutes. Sprinkle with parsley.

Opakapaka Caprice

A fabulous fish recipe from the Kahala Hilton kitchen. Opakapaka is the Hawaiian name for Red Snapper. Many Hawaiian fishes have double names. The Hawaiians believe their fish is doubly delicious. Any of your favorite fishes may be substituted in this recipe created by Executive Chef Martin Wyss.

Season	**4-6 ounce pieces of Opakapaka** with salt and pepper
Sauté	in **4 Tablespoons of butter**
Sauté	in a separate saucepan **1 shallot**, finely chopped in **4 Tablespoons butter**
Add	**6 medium, sliced fresh mushrooms** Dash of **salt** Dash of **pepper** Few drops of **lemon juice** **1/3 cup of white wine** Cook rapidly
Mix sauce	**4 Tablespoons of soft butter** with **2 Tablespoons of flour** and blend with mushroom
Add	**1/2 cup of Half and Half cream** Simmer for a few minutes Remove from the fire
Blend	in **1/cup whipped cream** **1 egg yolk**
Pour	sauce into four oblong dishes
Place	fish on sauce and top each serving with half a peeled banana which has been sliced lengthwise and slightly sautéed
Glaze	in oven and sprinkle with chopped parsley

Mary's Seafood Fettuccini

From Mary Delpech's kitchen comes this delicious recipe. A real gourmet dish! The black pepper is the secret.

Melt	**1 block butter**
Add	**2 cloves garlic**
Add	**1 lb. large shrimp**, peeled and deveined Cook until pinkish white
Remove	shrimp with slotted spoon and keep warm
Add	**1 lb. bay scallops** to garlic butter Cook until done. Remove and keep warm
Add	**1/2 block butter** to pan on medium to low heat
Mix	in **12 oz. sour cream** stirring slowly Cook for 2 minutes
Add	**2 teaspoons black pepper** **1 1/2 cup freshly grated parmesan cheese** Stir and cook for one minute
Add	cooked seafood to sauce
Boil	**1 lb. spinach fettuccini** according to directions
Pour	seafood over pasta. Stand 4-5 minutes to set before serving

Golden Shrimp Curry

Make with tender loving care. A wonderful party dish to make ahead. Serve out of a chafing dish and then relax and sit back for the compliments!

Put	**4 Tablespoons butter**
	2 Tablespoons curry
	2 Tablespoons flour into a 2 qt. size saucepan
	Cook together 3-5 minutes
Add	**3 cloves garlic**, smashed
	2 large onions, sliced
	2-3 inch piece ginger root, sliced
Cook	1/2 hour over low heat. Stir frequently
Add	**1 qt. frozen coconut milk.**
Cook	3 hours **over water**
Mash	ingredients through colander or wide meshed strainer
Discard	onions and ginger. Mixture will have consistency of thick cream
Add	salt to taste before serving
Add	**1 cup fresh cream** before serving
Add	2-3 lbs. boiled shrimp, 15 minutes before serving

If you have a fresh coconut and would like to make your own coconut milk – first, grate the coconut, put into saucepan and add 1 qt. fresh milk. Cook together for a half hour, being very careful not to burn the milk. Cool. Pour milk through a cheesecloth to squeeze out the coconut milk.

Condiments: Chopped hard boiled eggs, minced green onions, freshly grated coconut, mango chutney, raisins, chopped peanuts, chopped crisp bacon, sliced ripe bananas.

Boiled Shrimp

Prepare shrimp in the following manner for curry.

Place thawed shrimp in a large pot. In a separate kettle boil enough water to cover shrimp. Pour boiling water over shrimp and **cover pot tightly**. Steam shrimp in this manner for 15 minutes.

Drain and cool. Remove shell and black line from back of shrimp. Slice shrimp in half lengthwise and add to curry 15 minutes before serving.. Do not put the shrimp in too early, as the shrimp will toughen.

Choice Mango Chutney

Aunt Mary's Chutney has been sent to friends all over the world. They all agree it is by far the **very** best they have ever tasted! A must with curry.

Marinate	**12 cups half ripe mangos** sliced in large pieces in **6 cups sugar**, overnight
Boil	mangos in marinade for 30-40 minutes on low heat
Add	**1 1/4 cups vinegar** **1 1/4 cups water** **1/2 cup ginger root**, chopped fine **4 small red chili peppers** Remove seeds and chop fine **2 teaspoons cinnamon** **1 teaspoon powdered cloves** **1 clove garlic,** pressed **1 large onion**, sliced fine **1 teaspoon salt**
Simmer	over low heat for 1 hour or more Stir occasionally. Mangos will be glazed and syrup thick when done.
Fill	**6 sterilized pint jars**. Cover with melted **paraffin wax.**

Hawaiian Baked Crab

Wonderful for an elegant lunch.   Serve with chilled wine!

Sauté
1 tablespoon minced onion
1 tablespoon minced celery
1 tablespoon minced green pepper in
2 tablespoons butter, until tender
Remove pan from heat

Add
1/2 teaspoon salt
1/2 teaspoon freshly ground pepper
2-3 drops Tabasco sauce (more or less to taste)
2 Tablespoons evaporated milk
1 egg, slightly beaten
3 Tablespoons mayonnaise (more or less)
2 oz. sweet white wine
4 cans shredded crab meat. Fresh cooked crab is
better if you have it. Mix well

Spoon
into buttered serving dishes or shells

Top
with **buttered crumbs**

Bake
350 degrees for 20 minutes

Shrimp "Tahitienne"

The Tahitian lanai in Waikiki offers an excellent and varied cuisine. One
of our favorites is offered here.

Split
JUMBO shrimp in shell, down the back and devein

Pull
meat from shell up to the tail

Season
shrimp with:
Salt, pepper and melted butter

Broil
in hot oven (500 degrees) until shell turns pink

Serve
with melted **garlic butter**. (Press 1 clove garlic in 1
block melted butter)

Lomi Lomi Salmon

This may be served as a fish or salad course.

Wash, scale, and bone **salt salmon**

To	**1 cup salmon** (diced)
Add	**2 cups tomatoes** cut into small cubes **1/2 cup minced white onions**
Add	ice cubes and refrigerate until serving time
Add	**1/2 cup green onions** just before serving

Chinese Steamed Fish

Place	**1 lb. mullet or fish fillet** that has been scaled and cleaned in a steaming dish
Rub	**1/2 teaspoon salt** in the cavity of the fish
Sprinkle	**1 tablespoon pork fat**, finely chopped (opt) **1/2 inch piece ginger root**, finely chopped **1 good pinch of sugar** **2 tablespoons shoyu** over fish
Place	in a large pot
Bring	3 inches water in pot to boil. Cover tightly and steam 12-15 minutes. Remove to serving dish
Sprinkle	**3 stalks green onions**, finely chopped over fish
Heat	**2 tablespoons vegetable oil** with **1 clove garlic.** Remove garlic when brown
Pour	hot oil on fish over green onions

Quickie Tuna Burgers

This is really delicious. Children love it as a hamburger substitute.

Mix

2 cans tuna, well drained
1 Tablespoon minced onion
1 Tablespoon minced parsley
1 cup buttered crumbs
1/2 teaspoon dry mustard
½ teaspoon salt
Dash of freshly ground pepper
2 eggs
3 Tablespoons mayonnaise

Shape

into patties. Sauté in butter and serve on **toasted buns**

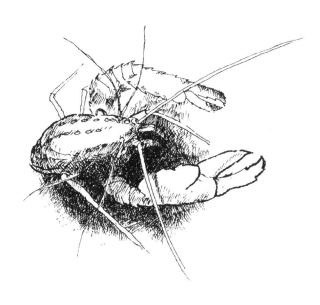

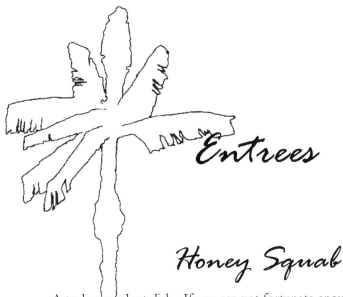

Honey Squab

A truly succulent dish. If you are not fortunate enough to have squab, chicken broilers will do. The flavor will not be the same if you try this on any larger size fowl.

Cut	**2 squabs** or **broilers** into serving pieces
Mix	**1/4 cup honey** **1/4 cup shoyu** **1/8 teaspoon Chinese Five Spices** **2 ozs. Sweet white wine** **1 inch piece of ginger root,** crushed Taste the marinade for sweetness Add more honey if necessary
Rub	marinade well into squabs and set aside for 30 minutes
Heat	**2-3 tablespoons vegetable oil** in a heavy pot that has a tight fitting cover
Sauté	squabs in hot oil, stirring quickly, until a dark, golden brown
Add	marinade. Cover tightly. Cook 15-20 minutes or until squabs are done
Serve	with hot steamed rice, Chinese Snow Peas

Almond Duck

Chef Wong Pui of the world renowned Waikiki Lau Yee Chai contributes his succulent Almond Duck. Topped with almonds and garnished with pineapple, maraschino cherries, pickled onions and papaya, it is a heavenly dish.

Thaw	**1 large Long Island duck**
Split	back of duck and place in pan
Into	the cavity add **1 tablespoon salt** **4 slices fresh ginger root** **1 preserved orange skin (Chinese Gopei)** **1/2 teaspoon Chinese Five Spices** **1 bunch chinese parsley** **6 stalks green onions** **2 ozs. Gin** **1 rice bowl of water** **Dash of white pepper**
Steam	for 2 hours in a tightly covered pot
Remove	bone
Dip	duck in cornstarch until well covered
Place	in freezer for 4 hours
Deep fry	the whole duck in got oil until a dark golden color
Cut	into1 inch pieces and place on platter
Cook	sauce made up with the following ingredients **1 cup vinegar** **1 cup brown sugar** **1 cup water** **3 Tablespoons cornstarch** **Catsup for color.** Cook until it thickens
Pour	over duck. **Sprinkle with finely chopped almonds.** Garnish with preserved **pickles and pineapple.**

46

Beachcombers's Spare Ribs

Donn Beach, the colorful entrepreneur of Waikiki and the famous International Market Place, shares his wonderful sparerib recipe for your enjoyment. These may also be served as pupus.

Mix
1 inch fresh ginger root, crushed
1/2 clove garlic
1/2 cup shoyu
3/4 cup sugar
1/2 cup catsup
2 oz. sherry
1/2 teaspoon salt

Rub into
3 lbs. SMALL ribs well. Marinate 3 hours or more

Bake
on rack at 325 degrees over shallow pan of water for 45 minutes. Baste occasionally.

Cut
into 2 inch riblets and serve.

Spareribs ala Apricot

This is a real finger-licking dish. Better double up on the recipe as everyone comes back for seconds and thirds.

Parboil
2-3 lbs. spareribs cut lengthwise into 6 inch pieces and 2 ribs wide. Drain well.

Rub
1 tablespoon rock salt well into ribs

Mix
1 inch piece ginger, sliced and crushed
1 clove garlic, crushed
1/3 cup shoyu
1 tablespoon sugar
2 ozs. White wine or whiskey
1/2 cup apricot jam

Marinate
ribs for 1 hour. Line baking dish with heavy foil and bake for 350 degrees for 45 minutes – 1 hour. Baste ribs with marinade. If ribs brown too quickly, cover dish with foil. Ribs may also be cooked over charcoal.

Easy Bar-B-Que Sauce

Great for left over pork or beef slices or as marinade for spareribs.

Stir	together **14 ozs. bottle of ketchup** **1/2 cup cider vinegar** **1/2 cup brown sugar firmly packed** **1 Tablespoon prepared mustard** **1 Tablespoon Worcestershire** **Dash of Tabasco** **1 large sweet onion sliced**
Pour	over cooked sliced pork or beef. Cover with foil and
Bake	at 350 degrees for 1 hour

Spareribs Bar-B-Que

Marinate	2-3 lbs par-boiled spare ribs for 1/2 hour in bar-b-que sauce
Put	in pan. Cover with foil and bake at 350 degrees for 1 hour
Uncover	ribs last 15 minutes

Sweet and Sour Spareribs

Parboil	**2 lbs. meaty spareribs**, cut in 2 inch pieces, by boiling in water just enough to cover for 15 minutes. Drain ribs well.
Sprinkle	**1 Tablespoon rock salt** over ribs and rub well
Mix	**1 Tablespoon white wine** **1/2 cup shoyu** **1 inch piece ginger,** sliced and smashed **1 clove garlic, smashed**, and marinate ribs. Let stand 1/2 hour, turning occasionally
Sauté	ribs golden brown in **2-3 Tablespoons hot peanut oil**

48

Sauce	**1 cup vinegar** **1/2 cup water** **1/4 cup pineapple juice**, drained from pineapple chunks **1/2 cup brown sugar** **1/2 cup white sugar** **1 Tablespoon cornstarch**
Mix	together well and cook until slightly thick
Add	ribs to sauce and simmer for 30 minutes Garnish with **pineapple chunks and chinese parsley.**

Bar-B-Qued Ham Slices

Mary Lapine offered this sumptuous bar-b-qued ham. Delicious hot or cold, it's a guaranteed company success. Serve it with an avocado-fruit salad and hot rolls.

Simmer	**1 cup pineapple juice** **1 cup apricot nectar** (1 small can) **1/4 cup prepared mustard** **1 teaspoon whole cloves** **2 Tablespoons brown sugar** **1/2 cup grenadine syrup** for 5 minutes and cool
Marinate	**2-4 slices center cut ham** 1 1/2 inches thick, for 2 hours or longer, turning occasionally. Trim off excess fat and score the edges of the ham before marinating.
Bar-b-que	over medium fire, not too close to the coals Do not sear or burn the ham
Cook	45 minutes
Slice	ham diagonally in 1/8 inch slices. Each ham slice serves 2-3 persons, depending on the size of the center cut.

Vinha D'Alhos

(Portuguese "Sauerbraten")

Skewer	**4 lb. pork butt well**
Mix	**3/4 cup dark cider vinegar** **1 1/2 cup water** **2-3 cloves garlic,** smashed **1-2 chili peppers** **1 teaspoon salt** **2 ozs. Whiskey or sherry** **1/4 cup chopped parsley**
Marinade	pork overnight, turning occasionally
Bake	at 350 degrees. Roast meat in liquid, turning meat as it browns. Add potatoes to gravy if desired. Roast 1 1/2 hours or 30 minutes per lb.
	Pork may be cubeb and boiled in the marinating liquid. When liquid boils down, add a little oil and fry. Makes wonderful pupus when served this way.

Hawaiian Laulaus

Use	**6 taro* leaves** for each lau-lau. Wash taro leaves and cut off stem tips.
Cut	**1-2 lbs. pork** into 1 1/2 inch squares
Sprinkle	with **rock salt**. Rub well into pork and set aside for a few minutes
Place	on stacked taro leaves **1 piece of butterfish** and the salted pork
Roll	one way in **a boned* ti leaf,** then roll the other way in a second ti leaf. Tie with string.
Steam	4-6 hours in a colander or on crossed sticks laid in the bottom of the pot. Sprinkle lau-laus with salted water before covering pot. Add more water as needed.

*Spinach leaves may be substituted for taro leaves

*Bone the ti leaves by partially cutting through the stiff rib on the underside of the leaf. Roll the leaf around the finger, stripping off the rib as it peels away. Foil may be used in place of the ti leaves.

Chinese Pork Hash

This is one of my husband's favorite dishes, and is usually on the menu once a week.

To	**1 lb. FRESH ground pork**
Add	**8-10 water chestnuts**, chopped medium **1 teaspoon cornstarch** **1 teaspoon sugar** **1 teaspoon shoyu** **1 teaspoon sweet white wine** **1/2 teaspoon salt** **1/8 teaspoon white pepper**. Stir well
Line	pork mixture on the sides and bottom of a steaming bowl, approximately 1 inch thick
Sprinkle	**1 Tablespoon Chinese sweet pickled cucumber** over the hash mixture (opt)
Steam	in a tightly covered pot over boiling water for 25-30 minutes
Serve	over hot rice with shoyu sauce

Pork Gravy for Fried Noodles

Soak	**1 large package or 2 small packages of dried black mushrooms** until tender Look for the large sized ones Remove the stems and discard. Slice in fine strips
Sauté	**1 1/2 lbs. fresh pork**, sliced in fine strips In 2 Tablespoons oil in a frying pan
Add	**1 teaspoon salt and sliced mushrooms**
Add	**1 can bamboo shoots**, sliced in thin strips
Add	**1 bunch green onions** cut in 2 inch pieces
Cook	for a few minutes then remove to a large pot
Swirl	a portion of the **2 cans chicken broth** in the frying pan Pour broth into pot and add enough water to measure 2 quarts
Add	**1 small ham bone** (optional)
Add	**2 rounded Tablespoons cornstarch** Mixed with **1/4 cup broth mixture**
Add	**1 teaspoon sugar**, more or less to taste **1 Tablespoon shoyu** **1 teaspoon oyster sauce** (optional) **Salt to taste** Simmer 1/2 hour or longer
Serve	over **Chinese style noodles**

Pork and Chicken Adobo

These two wonderful recipes were given to me by Mary Blanco. Typically Filipino family dishes, yet so palatable to western tastes. The Pork and Chicken Adobo is reminiscent of German Sauerbraten or Portuguese Vinga D'Alhos. Pansit, "which my children just love," says Mary, may yet be a version of Chinese Fried Rice, only substituting noodles for rice.

Cut	**1 1/2 lbs. spareribs or lean pork** **3-4 lbs. roasting chicken in 2 inch pieces** Save the chicken fat for frying
Mix	**2-3 cloves garlic,** vary to taste **1 bay leaf** **1/2 - 1 teaspoon black cracked pepper** **1/2 cup cider vinegar** **1 small chili pepper** (optional)
Marinate	3 hours. Remove chicken and pork from liquid and brown quickly over medium-high heat in melted chicken fat. Pour marinade over meat and simmer for 1 hour or until meat is tender. If vinegar boils away, add a little water. Salt to taste. Place on platter and decorate with pimento strips and parsley.

Pansit

Boil	**1 package saimin noodles** according to directions Drain
Brown	**1/2 lb. pork**, thinly sliced in **2 Tablespoons hot oil**
Add	**1 small round onion**, sliced Cook for a few minutes
Add	**1/2 lb. fresh shrimp**, cut in 1/2 inch pieces
Add	noodles which have been cut in 3-4 pieces
Add	**3 Tablespoons shoyu** or enough to give a golden brown color. Salt and pepper to taste. Place on platter and garnish with slices of **hard-boiled eggs, parsley and finely chopped green onions.**

Teriyaki Steak

Marinate	**2 lbs. ribeye or sirloin tip sliced 1/4 inch thick** in **2 ozs. Sweet white wine** **1/4 cup sugar** **1/2 cup shoyu** **1 inch ginger root,** thinly sliced, for 1-2 hours
Pan Fry	quickly in 2 Tablespoons hot oil, turning only once. The secret of good teriyaki is to be sure your meat is well marbled or streaked with fat. Be sure the steak is cooked very quickly.

Puleho Beef (Jerky)

Reminiscent of the old Hawaiian paniolo's (cowboys) Bar-B-Qued meat, this peppery beef is ono (delicious). Served with rice or poi.

Cut	**2-3 lbs. boneless chuck steak** into 1 1/2 inch by 3 inch pieces; put in broiler pan lined with foil
Sprinkle	lightly each piece with **rock salt** and rub in well
Mash	into small bowl **3-4 small red chili peppers** (quite hot) **2 cloves garlic** **1 teaspoon sugar**
Add	**3/4 cup shoyu,** mix well
Marinate	steak in sauce turning once or twice for 10 minutes
Broil	in pan on middle rack turning once. For medium rare steak, approximately 7 minutes on each side

Tournedos of Beef Tenderloin

Another of Michel's wonderful recipes. A quick one that you can marinate in the refrigerator and cook up in a few minutes. It's for that late dinner for two!

Mix	**1/2 teaspoon dried tarragon** with **1 oz. olive oil** **Salt and pepper** to taste
Marinate	eight 1 1/2 inch square pieces of beef tenderloin an hour before serving. If longer, keep beef in the marinade in the refrigerator.
Sauté	beef tenderloin in marinade until well browned
Add	**button mushrooms**
Serve	on toast with a spoonful of **béarnaise sauce**

Simple Béarnaise Sauce

Melt	**1/2 cup butter** until bubbly but not brown
Whip	at high speed in mixer or blender **3 egg yolks** **2 Tablespoons lemon juice** **1 oz. dry white wine** **1/2 teaspoon minced shallots** **1/2 teaspoon minced parsley** **1/2 teaspoon dried tarragon leaves** **1/2 teaspoon salt** **Dash of fresh ground pepper**
Pour	in hot melted butter slowly
Serve	immediately or place container in 2 inches of hot, not boiling water, until ready to serve

Beef Sukiyaki

This recipe may be varied by substituting pork or chicken, or using half beef and pork.

Sauté in	**2 Tablespoons butter** **1 1/2 lbs. sirloin tip** or any tender cut of beef, Cut in strips, until brown
Add	**1 gobo**, sliced julienne (optionsl) **1 medium round onion**, sliced; cook until tender
Add	**8-10 stalks green onions**, cut in2 inch sections **1 tofu** cut in cubes (bean curd) **1 can sukiyaki no tomo** (vegetables consisting of mushrooms and bamboo shoots)
Mix	**1 cup shoyu** **1/2 cup water** **1/2 cup sugar** (more or less to taste) **1 jigger sake or white wine**. Add to meat
	Cook together 15-20 minutes. Serve on hot steamed rice.

Beef in Shoyu Sauce

This is one of the children's favorites. They call it "Shoyu Meat."

Slice	**1 1/2 lbs. tender cut of meat** into thin strips
Put a	**1/2 inch ginger root** into press and squeeze juice over meat
Sprinkle	**2 Tablespoons cornstarch** **2 Tablespoons sweet white wine** **2 Tablespoons shoyu** **1 teaspoon salt** **A dash of pepper** over meat and rub in well
Heat	**2 Tablespoons oil** in heavy pan over medium heat
Add	**1/4 cup water** to the meat for extra gravy **Salt** to taste and serve over hot rice

Beef Tomato with Green Peppers

Use the Beef in Shoyu Sauce recipe. Before adding the water, however, quarter a large ripe tomato, a sliced green pepper, and 1/2 onion quartered. Stir it into the meat. After a few minutes of cooking, ad the 1/4 cup of water for the extra gravy.

Korean Broiled Meat

Cut	**5 lbs. rib eye, sirloin tip**, or **prime short ribs** into pieces
Marinate	meat in the following sauce for 1 hour
	1 1/2 cups shoyu
	1/2 cup vegetable oil
	1/2 teaspoon black pepper
	1 heaping Tablespoon sesame seeds
	1 Tablespoon sugar
	4 stalks of chopped green onions
	5 cloves garlic, crushed
	1 inch piece ginger root, crushed
	1 teaspoon sesame oil
Broil	over charcoal

Roasted Sesame Seeds

Wash	**1-2 packages of sesame seeds** thoroughly several times
Drain	well in colander, shaking to dry
Place	in pan, spreading evenly
Roast	in 350 degrees over until seeds are puffed and brown (10-15 minutes). Stir the seeds occasionally
Crush	seeds while still warm, salting lightly
Store	in jar and refrigerate. Keeps indefinitely

Hamburgers Diane

Only one word – HEAVENLY!

Shape	**1 lb. fresh ground chuck** into 3/4 -1 inch thick patties
Press	**fresh ground pepper** well on both sides of patty Let stand for 30 minutes
Sprinkle	**light layer of salt** in heavy pan Heat until salt turns light brown
Place	patties in pan and brown well on one side. Turn.
Place	**1 Teaspoon Worcestershire sauce** **1 teaspoon lemon juice** **1 pat of butter** on each patty When patty is well browned on the under side,
Pour	**1/4 cup brandy** over all patties
Turn	heat down and light brandy
Spoon	brandy over all the patties and serve immediately

Spaghetti Florentine

The Frank Padgetts discovered this dish in Florence, Italy. Remembering the wonderful flavor, they adapted this recipe to their tastes and have made it a family favorite.

Heat	a large casserole in the oven while preparing the following ingredients
	1 1/2 cups grated mozzarella cheese, **12 large pitted olives, chopped** **3/4 cup minced parsley** **2-3 eggs, well beaten** **1 large whole pimento**, sliced in strips

Boil	one 16 oz. package long spaghetti in 2 quarts of salted water with 1 Tablespoon olive oil 1 clove garlic
Cook	al dente. Drain and place in heated casserole.
Add	mozzarella cheese, olives, parsley to the spaghetti and fold in the beaten eggs. Salt to taste
Garnish	with pimento strips. Serve immediately

Spaghetti Al Dente

If your spaghetti isn't cooked properly, the best sauce can't do anything for it. Here are some hints for cooking spaghetti.

1. Water must be boiling rapidly.

2. Add 2 Tablespoons vegetable oil

3. Add 1 Tablespoon rock salt.

4. Add spaghetti and stir. When water comes to a boil again set timer for 8 minutes. Be sure to test when the timer goes off.

5. Drain immediately, adding butter and stir. Serve immediately.

An old fashioned testing method: if a piece of spaghetti is thrown at a wall and it sticks – it's done.

Herbed French Bread

Mix	1 teaspoon oregano with 1 block softened butter
Spread	on diagonally sliced French bread
Bake	350 degrees oven until hot and crisp

Spaghetti Meat Sauce

Another family favorite. Put it on in the morning and forget about cooking the rest of the day.

Have the butcher grind together twice:

> **1 lb. round or ground chuck**
> **1/2 lb. veal**
> **1/4 lb. pork**

Sauté
> **1 clove garlic** in
> **2 Tablespoons olive oil**.
> When garlic browns, remove and

Add
> **1 medium onion** minced and cook until tender

Add
> meat to onions and cook until meat is brown but still slightly pink

Add
> **1 can tomato paste**   Cook 15 minutes

Add
> **1 can solid pack tomatoes, large size**
> **1 can tomato puree**
> **1 teaspoon sweet basil**
> **1 teaspoon oregano**
> **1 bay leaf**
> **1 teaspoon salt**
> **1 teaspoon sugar**
> **1/4 cup red wine (optional)**
> **1 can button mushrooms**

Cook
> together, uncovered until sauce thickens.
> About 1 1/2 – 2 hours. Salt to taste
> And serve over spaghetti cooked al dente.

Taco Casserole Ole!

A spicy, easy to prepare one dish meal. Quite peppery, definitely not for weak stomachs, but oh, so good!

Place	**1 small package taco chips** in long oblong pan
Brown	**2 lbs. lean hamburger meat** or **ground turkey** and place on top of the chips
Mix	**1 can cream of mushroom soup** **1 can cream of chicken soup** **2 small cans chopped green peppers (chilies)** **1 cup milk** **1 can enchilada sauce (mild or hot)** in same pan. Pour over ground meat
Top with	**1 cup grated cheddar cheese**
Heat	at 350 or 375 degrees till cheese melts and all is hot
Serve	with green salad and extra corn chips
	Try crumbled tofu in place of the meat

Children's Special Goulash

A one-pan dinner, a favorite request on dad's and mom's night out.

Heat	**2 Tablespoons oil**
Sauté	**1 small minced onion** **2 stalks minced celery**
Add	**1-1 1/2 lbs. ground chuck steak**
Cook	until meat is browned but still light pink
Add	**3 medium potatoes**, pared and cut in 1/2 inch cubes

Add	**1/2 cup water.** Cover and simmer for 15 minutes.

Add	**1 can tomato soup** **Salt and pepper to taste**
Cover	and simmer 10-15 minutes, stirring occasionally
Serve	with a green salad and crunchy French bread

Beef Corn Niblets

These two recipes are perfect for teenage cooks and busy mothers who have only minutes to put together a family meal.

Sauté	in hot* salted pan **2 lbs. ground chuck** until lightly brown DO NOT OVERCOOK

Add	**2 cups ketchup** **1 medium can corn niblets** **1/2 teaspoon sugar** **Dash of pepper**
Cook	10-15 minutes
Serve	over rice

*Sprinkle layer of salt on bottom of pan
Put in meat when a few drops of water sizzle in pan.

Swedish Meat Balls

This has yummy gravy—served over rice or noodles with green salad. A real family pleaser.

Mix	in large bowl **2 lbs. ground chuck** **1 egg** **1/4 cup evaporated milk** **1/2 teaspoon salt.** Roll in 1 inch to 1 1/2 inch size balls
Sauté	in large salted pan until well browned on all sides

Stir in	**1 can cream of mushroom soup**
	With fork until blended with meat juice

Add	**1/4 teaspoon black pepper**
	1/4 teaspoon allspice

Simmer	for 15-20 minutes. Add milk if gravy becomes too thick.

Sherried Beef

Easy. One dish main course, great for gravy lovers. Serve over steamed rice or egg noodles.

Combine	**3 lbs. stewing beef, cut in 1 1/2 inch cubes**
	2 cans cream of mushroom soup
	3/4 cup sherry wine
	1/2 package dry onion soup
	1 can whole mushrooms

Place	in a large casserole, cover with foil

Bake	in pre-heated oven at 325 degrees for 3 hours

Oven Casserole Stew

I met Vitoria Forrest early one morning at Kress's lunch counter in Kailua. She was a retired school teacher and she passed on one of her favorite recipes. Pop it in the oven before leaving the house and return home to a delicious stew. You'll love it. The secret is the fresh ginger.

Cut	**chuck steak** into 2 inch squares
	Roll in **flour, salt and pepper**

Put	in bottom of deep casserole dish

Add	**1 large onion in wedges**
	1 large potato cut into squares
	3-4 carrots cut into pieces
	1/2 inch piece of fresh ginger, finely chopped.
	(This is the secret ingredient)

Mix	**3/4 cup catsup**
	1 cup water. Pour over meat and vegetables

Cover   and bake 180 degrees all day or 300 degrees for 3 hours

Veal Parmigiana

This makes a wonderful company dinner. Prepare it ahead of time. Pop
it in the oven when the guests arrive. Relax until dinner.

Heat	**3 Tablespoons olive oil** in saucepan
Sauté	**1 medium minced onion** with **1 clove garlic**, pressed; until golden
Stir in	**2-8 oz. cans tomato sauce** **1/4 can water** **1 teaspoon oregano** **1/8 teaspoon pepper** **1 Tablespoon chopped parsley**
Cover	and simmer 10 minutes
Combine	**1/2 cup parmesan cheese** with **1/2 cup fine dry bread crumbs**
Dip	**6 slices veal** 1/4 inch thick in **1 egg** slightly beaten. Dip in crumb mixture.
Sauté	veal in oil, turning only once
Pour	1/2 sauce mixture in bottom of baking dish Lay browned veal in sauce
Alternate	**1 package sliced mozzarella cheese**, with veal
Pour	remaining sauce over veal
Sprinkle	**2 Tablespoons parmesan cheese** over veal
Bake	in 350 degree oven for 25-30 minutes. Cook longer if you have more than 2 layers. Cover casserole with foil to keep sauce from drying out.

Veal Scaloppini

This is the simplest way I have found to cook scaloppini. It is smooth to the taste and delicious with plain steamed rice. Be sure to serve a chilled rose wine.

Season	**1 1/2 lbs. thinly sliced veal** with **Salt** and freshly **ground pepper**
Sauté	veal in **2-4 Tablespoons butter** until brown
Pour	**2 Tablespoons sweet white wine** Stir and remove meat from the pan
Add	**1/2 cup sliced fresh mushrooms** or 1 small can **1 scant teaspoon tomato paste** **1 Tablespoon guava jelly** or **red currant jelly** **3 Tablespoons Sautérne** or **dry white wine** **Dash of cayenne pepper** (easy, as it is very hot)
Dissolve	**2 Tablespoons cornstarch** in **1 1/2 cups chicken broth** (canned) and Add to mushrooms Season to taste with **salt and pepper**
Return	veal to sauce and simmer for 15-20 minutes

For quick scaloppini, veal can be served after the first three steps only topping the veal with buttered mushrooms. Cook the veal a little longer in the butter wine sauce.

Lamb Chops A La Gus

"Gus" Guslander, gourmet chef, prepared this NEW YEAR PICNIC favorite with great joie de vivre. Absolutely delicious!

Sprinkle	**six 3/4 inch rib or loin lamb chops** liberally with, **garlic salt** and **black pepper**

65

Mix	**2 teaspoons dry mustard** with **4 Tablespoons shoyu** into a thin paste
Marinate	for 15-20 minutes turning chops 2 to 3 times
Grill	on well prepared bed of charcoal
Slosh	**dry French vermouth** on chops before serving

Chinese Walnut Chicken

Spread	**1 cup of shelled walnuts** on an Ungreased baking sheet and bake in A 500 degree oven for 3-4 minutes
Remove	skins by rubbing walnuts in a towel
Fry	in **2 inches of vegetable oil** until golden brown. Drain and sprinkle lightly with salt. Put aside until ready to use.
Bone	**one 1 lb. package chicken breasts** and dice into 1 inch squares
Marinate	chicken with: **2 Tablespoons shoyu** **1/2 teaspoon sugar** **1 Tablespoon vegetable oil** **2 teaspoons cornstarch** **2 Tablespoons sweet white wine** **2-3 drops ginger root juice.** Rub chicken pieces well. Let stand for 30 minutes.
Heat	**2 Tablespoons vegetable oil** in heavy pan
Sauté	**1 package snow peas** (washed and dried) and remove from pan when bright green
Add	chicken and cook quickly, stirring rapidly for 2 minutes. Chicken meat will turn white. Be sure not to overcook.
Add	**1 small can water chestnuts,** sliced **Snow peas, walnuts, and 1/4 cup water** **Season with salt and white pepper** Cook 3 minutes. Serve immediately

Chicken Wings Oriental

This is the recipe entered in the 1963 Mrs. America Contest. A family favorite and so simple to prepare.

Disjoint   **2 lbs. chicken wings** at the first large bone

Sauté   **1 inch ginger root**, sliced in
1/2 block of butter, until transparent

Add   chicken wings and fry until the skin color changes

Add   **2 ozs. Sweet white wine** and cover tightly for a few seconds until wine permeates chicken

Add   **1 cup shoyu**
1/4 cup sugar (more or less to taste)
1/2 cup water or chicken broth

Simmer   30-45 minutes. Serve over hot steamed rice with hot towels for finger-wiping.

Bar-B-Qued Chicken

This chicken is best cooked over charcoal. Be sure to buy chicken with a deep, yellow skin color. I find chicken boxed in the South is the best.

Put   **5 lbs. chicken thighs** into a large pot

Add   **2 inch ginger root,** sliced
1 1/2 cups shoyu
2/3 cups sugar
2 ozs. Sweet white wine

Marinate   in sauce for 4 or more hours
Stir chicken in sauce as the pieces defrost

Cook   over hot coals turning frequently
Be sure to allow about 4 pieces per person

Oven Baked Chicken

Disjoint	**one 3 lb. fryer** and place in baking dish
Sprinkle	**salt and freshly ground pepper**
Pour	**1/4 cup melted butter over chicken** or dot well with slices of butter
Bake	375 degrees oven for 1 hour. Baste occasionally
Add	**1/2 cup cream** 15 minutes before chicken is done
Serve	with steamed rice. Spoon sauce over chicken Serve with Chinese snow peas

Chinese Chicken Rice

Steaming hot, it has a "can't wait" aroma about it.

Marinate	**1 1/2 cups shredded or cubed chicken meat** in **5 Tablespoons shoyu** **5 Tablespoons sweet white wine** for a few minutes
Remove	chicken and sauté in **2 Tablespoons hot oil**. Remove chicken
Add	a portion of **4 cups chicken broth** (canned) to the pan to take up the drippings
Wash	**3 cups white rice** and place in medium sauce pan
Add	chicken broth and shoyu marinade to rice
Bring	to a boil. Lower to medium heat until broth is absorbed. Stir in chicken quickly, cover and cook over low heat for 20 minutes.

Chicken A La Esta

From the kitchen of Esta Chaplain comes this spicy chicken with a golden brown glaze, simmering in a pungent, sweet and sour sauce.

Place · · · · **5 lbs. chicken thighs** in an uncovered dish
Do not overlap as chicken will not brown evenly

Mix · · · · **1-8 oz. jar of guava jelly**
1 Tablespoon cornstarch
1 cup water
1/4 cup lime juice or lemon
2 Tablespoons Worcestershire sauce
1 oz. sherry
4 drops ginger juice (or put 1/2 inch ginger root in presser)
1 1/2 teaspoons allspice
3 teaspoons salt
1/4 teaspoon black pepper in saucepan
And bring to a boil. Simmer 5 minutes

Pour · · · · sauce over chicken and bake in450 degree oven for 15 minutes. Reduce heat to 350 degrees and bake for another 45 minutes. Baste frequently. If sauce thickens, add water.

Coq au Vin

A simplified version of the French dish. Elegant enough for the most discriminating guests.

Place · · · · **2-3 lbs. chicken thighs** in baking pan
Sprinkle **salt and pepper** on thighs and dot with butter

Place · · · · thinly sliced **onions** on each thigh

Bake · · · · at 350 degree for 1 hour

Mix · · · · **1 can cream of mushroom soup**
2 Tablespoons white port wine
1/4 cup light sour cream
1/2 cup milk (opt)

Pour · · · · over chicken. Bake an additional 20 minutes

Miriam's Chicken Kiev

Not as difficult as you would think. You can serve this proudly on you best china.

Butterfly	**4 chicken breasts**, skinned, boned and pounded flat
Sprinkle	**1 Tablespoon chopped green onions** **1 Tablespoon chopped parsley** over cutlets
Cut	**1 block butter** (well chilled) into 8 sticks
Place	**a stick of butter** at the end of each cutlet Roll the cutlet, tucking in sides. Press end to seal well.
Dust	each cutlet roll with **flour**
Dip	in **2 well beaten eggs** then into fine, **dry bread crumbs**
	CHILL THOROUGHLY for at least an hour
Fry	chicken rolls in deep, hot oil (340°) about 5 minutes or until golden brown
Serve	with Mushroom Sauce and garnish with **lemon wedges and parsley**

Mushroom Sauce

Melt	**3 Tablespoons butter**
Add	**1/2 cup fresh sliced mushrooms** Sprinkle with **1 Tablespoon flour**
Cook	over medium heat, stirring occasionally, 8-10 minutes
Add	**1 teaspoon shoyu**
Stir	in **3/4 cup light cream** slowly
Cook	and stir until mixture bubbles and thickens. Season to taste

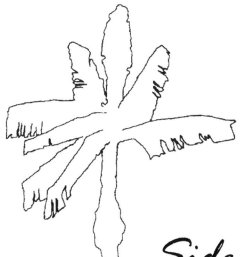

Side Orders

Kim (Broiled Seaweed)

This is seaweed prepared Korean style. The children love it! Fun to take on picnics!

1 package Nori (seaweed)

Sesame oil

Brush sesame oil on both sides of nori.. Sprinkle lightly with salt. Toast under broiler turning once as the nori changes color and starts to curl. Tear into 4 equal parts. Roll it around a ball of hot rice and eat it with your fingers.

Artichokes by Buzz

Buzz Schneider, of Buzz's Steak and Lobster; share his secret on the preparation of artichokes. The artichokes must not be cooked longer than 40 minutes. Fixed this way, they are fit for a king!

Wash	**3 artichokes** thoroughly in cold water
Trim	stems flush with the bottom of the artichokes
Pour	enough water into a deep pot to completely cover the artichoke
Add	**1/2 cup olive oil** **1/2 cup red wine vinegar** **2 cloves garlic,** crushed
Bring	water to boil
Immerse	artichokes and set timer immediately for 40 minutes
Serve	with **mayonnaise**, hot or cold

Chinese Vegetable Omelet

Sauté	**1 clove garlic** in **1 Tablespoon vegetable oil** until golden Remove
Add	**1/4 cup finely sliced ham** **1/2 cup finely sliced bamboo shoots** (optional) Cook few minutes. Remove from pan
Beat	**6 eggs** Add ham and bamboo shoots to eggs Mix well
Add	**3 stalks green onions**, finely chopped
Pour	egg mixture to cover bottom of pan Cook until egg sets, turning patty once Remove to platter. Cook the remaining egg mixture in the same manner. Serve with shoyu sauce.

Minced Broccoli

Waikiki Lau Yee Chai offers this piece de resistance! A fabulous blend of vegetables. Once you taste this you will never forget it.

Heat	**2 Tablespoons vegetable oil** with **1 clove garlic** until garlic is brown Remove the garlic
Sauté	**1/2 lb. lean, fresh pork,** finely chopped **1/2 teaspoon salt**
Add	**1 lb. broccoli stalks,** washed and finely chopped **2 stalks celery,** finely chopped **12-15 water chestnuts,** finely chopped
Cook	until broccoli turns bright green
Add	sauce made of the following ingredients **1 Tablespoon shoyu** **1 rounded teaspoon sugar** **1 rounded Tablespoon cornstarch** **1 oz. gin** **1/2 inch piece ginger root,** crushed Before adding sauce, squeeze juice from ginger and remove Dash of **white pepper** **1/4 cup chicken broth** or **water**
Add	**2 eggs,** stirring very quickly. Remove from heat as soon as mixture binds together.
Serve	On bed of leaf lettuce (butter or manoa) Garnish with **1/4 cup finely chopped peanuts**

Papoulu (Bananas)

Two Farden family recipes from the island of Maui are the Papoulu, Hawaiian baked bananas, and the Koele Palau, sweet potato balls. In choosing the bananas, look for the orange-yellow variety, which are fat with rounded ends. Buy them when they are spotted with black.

Boil	**bananas** until the skin starts to split Press the bananas from the bottom, out of their skins
Place	in baking dish, dot generously with **Butter, brown sugar and lemon juice**
Bake	30-40 minutes in moderate 350 degree oven
	Chinese or Bluefield bananas may be used. Do not boil this variety. They also may be sautéed in butter and brown sugar for 15 minutes, with juice of 1 orange.

Koele Palau
(Sweet Potato Balls)

Mash	**yams or sweet potatoes**
Add	**1 egg** and mix well
Add	heated **coconut milk,** just enough to hold the potatoes together
Add	**brown sugar** to taste
Roll	into a ball. Insert a **marshmallow** into the center of each ball
Roll	in crushed **cornflakes**
Deep fry	until lightly browned
Serve	with ham, turkey or chicken
	*Try chopping a little candied ginger and sprinkling it over the bananas or mixing a little with the yams

Chinese Snow Peas

Wash   **1 package of Chinese snow peas**, break off tips, dry

Sauté   peas in **2 Tablespoons vegetable oil** until bright green in color. Stir quickly

Add   **1 small can sliced water chestnuts** or
8-10 fresh peeled water chestnuts
1 small can sliced button mushrooms, drained

Season   to taste with salt and pepper. Do not overcook

Chinese Steamed Rice

Wash   **1 1/2 cups extra fancy California rice with
1 1/2 cups long grain rice** Drain water well

Add   **3 cups water** to rice. Place over high heat

Keep   saucepan uncovered until water comes to a boil.
Lower heat to medium and cook until water is absorbed

Cover   and steam on low heat for 15-20 minutes. It is
Important to watch the rice carefully during the first
part of cooking to avoid burning

Chinese Fried Rice

Sauté   **6 slices bacon** cut in 1/2 inch strips, until half cooked

Add   **2-2 1/2 cups cooked rice** and stir until glazed and
separated

Add   **2 Tablespoons shoyu** or enough to give
the rice a deep golden color

Add   **4 green onions** chopped fine, stirring well
1/2 cup frozen green peas

Add   **1 egg**, stirring quickly

Add   bits of **ham, pork, chicken, beef.**

Mother's Baked Beans

Red kidney beans prepared in a bean pot. Tasty and delicious, this dish is perfect for any meat. Economical too. (Serves 8)

Fix	**1 lb. package of red kidney beans** according to directions. Drain and save bean stock
Lay	**6-8 bacon strips** on the bottom and up the side of The bean pot or casserole. Work in a circle letting the Ends fall to the outside of the pot.
Mix	into the beans **8 oz. can tomato soup** **1 Tablespoon Worcestershire sauce** **1 teaspoon salt** **1/2 teaspoon dry mustard** **1/2 cup light brown sugar**, firmly packed **3 stalks green onions** cut in 2 inch pieces **1 bay leaf** **1 clove garlic**, pressed or finely chopped
Put	beans into bean pot or casserole
Bury	**1 medium onion**, quartered, in the beans
Add	**1 cup bean stock** Fold in the bacon ends
Bake	400 degrees until mixture boils, then 300 degrees – 4 hours covered Uncover the last 1/2 hour to brown

Breads

Famous Kona Inn Banana Bread

I was delighted to find retired Chef Max Mori of Kona Inn fame. His Banana Bread has always been a family favorite. This particular recipe has always been in great demand, so here it is as dictated y Chef Mori himself.

Cream	**2 cups sugar** **1 cup butter**
Add	**3 large or 4 medium eggs**
Mash	**6 ripe bananas**, Chinese or Bluefield
Sift	**2 1 /2 cups cake flour** **1 teaspoon salt** **2 teaspoons bottled baking soda** Sift these ingredients 3 TIMES
Alternate	bananas with flour mixture
Mix	ONLY until blended
Pour	into two 1 lb. loaf pans which have been Lightly greased and wax-lined
Bake	at 350 ° for 60 minutes or longer

Ono Banana Muffins

Cream	2 cups sugar 1 cup butter
Add	6 ripe mashed bananas 4 well beaten eggs
Sift	2 1/2 cups flour 1 teaspoon salt 2 teaspoons baking soda. Add to banana mixture
Pour	into greased muffin pans
Bake	at 350° for 15-20 minutes

Deluxe Mango Bread

Mix	all following ingredients together in a large bowl 2 cups flour 1 1/2 cups sugar 2 teaspoons cinnamon 2 teaspoons baking soda 1/2 teaspoon salt 1/2 cup chopped macadamia nuts 1/2 cup unsweetened shredded coconut
Make	a well in the flour mixture
Add	3 large eggs, slightly beaten 1 teaspoon vanilla 1 cup safflower oil Mix well
Add	2 cups diced mango Stir until well blended
Fill	two 1 lb. oiled and wax paper lined loaf pans with mixture
Bake	at 350° for 55 minutes. Cool before slicing. Can be wrapped in foil and frozen.

78

Buttermilk Pancakes

Light as a feather! These pancakes will literally melt in your mouth! I suggest topping them with coconut syrup for a Hawaiian taste treat!

Sift	**1 cup flour** **3/4 teaspoon baking soda** **1/4 teaspoon salt** **1 Tablespoon sugar**
Add	**1 1/2 cup buttermilk**
Separate	**2 eggs**. Beat **egg whites** until stiff
Beat	**yolks** until creamy and add to mixture Fold in egg whites until just blended
Heat	pan and test for correct temperature *Test pan by sprinkling with water. When water beads and moves, pan is ready.

Crunchy Drop Biscuits

This recipe never fails. Perfect for a weekend morning brunch. Scrumptious served hot with butter and honey!

Sift	**3 cups pastry flour** **1/2 teaspoon salt** **1/2 teaspoon sugar** **6 teaspoons baking powder**
Cut in	**6 Tablespoons butter**
Add	**1 large beaten egg** **1 cup milk** Stir with fork making sure all the flour mixture is moistened. If mixture is a little dry, add 1 Tablespoon of milk until four mixture is sticky but not soft
Drop	by teaspoon onto greased cookie sheet
Bake	at 450° 10-12 minutes or until golden brown

Cold Oven Popovers

A Sunday morning treat. Tested and tried for 10 years, this simple recipe has never failed.

Beat	into bowl **2 large eggs** Beat well with fork
Add	**1 cup milk** **1 cup flour** **1/2 teaspoon salt** Beat with fork. Disregard lumps
Pour	into 6 well greased muffin cups
Put	info COLD oven
Turn	to 450°. Bake exactly for 30 minutes, TURN OFF oven, prick popovers, return to oven for 10 minutes

Taro Puff Biscuits

Irmgard Farden Aluli, well known Island composer, remembers these Taro Puff Biscuits being serves in her family home, PUA MANA, on the island of Maui. Be sure to serve these with "gobs of butter." In selecting the taro, look for the dark grey or "purple" taro root.

Peel	**taro root** and cut into quarters
Boil	taro root until done, 30-45 minutes. Test with fork
Mash	hot taro root and add **1 teaspoon baking powder** **1/2 teaspoon salt** to each cup of mashed taro
Roll or	pat on floured board. Roll into balls.
Deep fry	until lightly browned and puffed. Taro biscuits may be baked in 450° oven for 12-15 minutes. Irmgard says it's best when deep fried. Serve immediately.

Mexicali Cornbread

A zippy addition to a "pot luck" supper. Compliments of Pat Bryan.

Mix   together
16 oz. can cream corn
3/4 cup milk
1/3 cup melted butter
2 eggs slightly beaten

Add   **1 cup corn meal**
1/2 teaspoon soda
1 teaspoon salt

Pour   half batter into a 9 x 9 inch square pan

Spread   with **1 – 4 oz. can Ortega green chilies** chopped and seeded
3/4 cup shredded cheddar cheese

Spread   rest of batter and
3/4 cup shredded cheese

Bake   at 400° for 45 minutes

Etta Holland's Spoon Bread

This is a marvelous recipe for spoonbread made with grits. Etta says this recipe originated in North Carolina.

Mix   **2 cups cooked grits** with
2 Tablespoons butter

Add   **2 large eggs**, one at a time, beating
well after each addition

Add   **1 teaspoon baking powder**
1 teaspoon salt, scant
2 Tablespoons minced parsley

Add   **2 cups milk**, stir well. Pour into buttered casserole

Bake   at 350° for 30 minutes. If you use a small dish and
Batter is quite deep, bake for 45 minutes.

Jo's Portuguese Malasada

These malasadas are the very best I have ever tasted. The doughnuts are light and fluffy and delicately flavored. The trouble with this recipe is that I am sure you will eat far too many!

Dissolve	**2 packages yeast** in **1/4 cup warm water** with **1/2 teaspoon granulated sugar**
Sift	**6 cups pastry flour**
Add	**1/2 block soft butter** **6 large well beaten eggs** **1/2 cup granulated sugar** **1/4 teaspoon salt**
Add	**1 cup evaporated milk** diluted with **1 cup water**
Mix well	cover and let rise 1 1/2 – 2 hours or until doubled
Punch	dough down in a circular motion. Let rise again. About 1/2 hour or longer.
Dip	hands in a little oil. Take a small amount of dough in both hands spreading it between fingers to form irregular circles.
Drop	carefully into 1-1 1/2 quarts hot oil. A Chinese frying pan is excellent for this. Turn doughnut as the edges turn a golden brown.
Drain	on absorbent paper. Before serving, dip in following syrup
Boil	**3 cups granulated sugar** with **1 1/2 cups water** for 5 minutes
Yields	about 4 dozen doughnuts
	Be sure to have oil at correct frying temperature. Test by dropping a dry crust of bread in oil. Oil is ready when bread turns golden brown.

Grandmother Santos' Portuguese Sweet Bread

This recipe, from the Island of Maui, is two generations old. How well I remember as a little girl, eating this marvelous bread, hot from the oven with lots of butter.

Mix
1 sifter pastry flour (4 cups)
4 packages yeast, melted in 1/4 cup warm water
1 teaspoon salt
2 Tablespoons sugar
1 cup warm potato water
Let rise 1 hour

Add
3 sifters pastry four (12 cups)
3 1/2 cups sugar
1 teaspoon salt
8 eggs beaten well
1 mashed potato
1 cup warm milk

Knead
into mixture
1 cup Crisco
1 cup butter
1 cup raisins

Knead until mixture peels off your hands and feels smooth and elastic. Put into large greased bowl and let rise until double in a warm place. Take a piece and roll by hand into a thick rope and knot loosely. Place in round greased cake pans. Let rise until double. Bake 350° 45 minutes to 1 hour.

Delicious Coffee Cake

Light as a feather, simple to make and wonderful to taste. Re-heated in foil, this coffee cake with taste just as delicious on the second day.

Sift	**1/2 cup sugar** **1 1/2 cups pastry flour** **1/4 teaspoon salt** **3 teaspoons baking powder**
Cut	**1 block butter** Into the four mixture until pea size
Add	**1 well beaten egg** **1/2 cup milk**
Stir	lightly until JUST BLENDED
Spread	1/2 of batter into well greased 8 x 8 pan Spread 1/2 of following filling over batter
Filling	**1/2 cup brown sugar**, firmly packed **2 teaspoons cinnamon** **2 Tablespoons flour** **3 Tablespoons melted butter**. Mix well
Spread	rest of batter over filling. Top with remaining filling and
Sprinkle	**1/4 cup chopped nuts** over batter
Bake	at 375° for 25 minutes

Desserts

Dream Delights

Mary Lane's delectable goodie is a family favorite. You will love it!

Cream   **3/4 cup softened butter** with
3/4 cup powdered sugar

Add   **1 1/2 cup flour**
Beat until smooth, using electric mixer. Spread in a 9 x 13 pan

Bake   at 400 ° for 10-12 minutes until golden brown. Cool

Mix   **1 3/4 cup plus 2 Tablespoons light brown sugar**
3 well beaten eggs. Beat until light

Add   in following order
3 Tablespoons flour
1 1/2 teaspoons baking powder
1 1/2 cup unsweetened shredded coconut
1 1/2 cup chopped walnuts
3/4 teaspoon vanilla
3/4 teaspoon almond extract
Mix together lightly

Spread   over top of crust

Bake   at 350 ° for 30 minutes
Cool and cut into 1 1/2 inch squares

Baklava

An authentic Greek recipe shared by Eleni. A real gourmet dessert and surprisingly simple to make.

Preheat	oven to 350°
Mix	**2 cups chopped walnuts and almonds** **1/2 cup bread crumbs** **1/2 cup sugar** **1/2 teaspoon cinnamon** **1/2 teaspoon cloves**
Melt	**1 1/2 cups sweet butter** (unsalted)
Grease	12 x 16 inch pan with sweet butter (unsalted)
Layer	**filo leaves** two pieces at a time in a pan
Brush	with melted butter
Spread	nut mixture over filo leaves. Repeat layers Leave 5 filo leaves for the top
Brush	with remaining butter
Cut	into triangles
Bake	in 350° oven for approximately 1 hour
	Pour following syrup over cooled Baklava

Baklava Syrup

Boil	for 15 minutes **4 cups sugar** **2 cups water** **Juice of 1 large lemon**
Pour	hot syrup over cooled Baklava

Melt Away Tarts

Put	in bowl **1 cup flour**
Cut	in **1/4 lb. butter** **one 3 oz. package of cream cheese**
Roll	and chill in refrigerator for one hour
Roll	thin and cut into circles
Put	**1/2 teaspoon of any type of jelly** into the centers
Fold	and seal edges with water to make a crescent shape
Bake	in preheated over of 375° for 10-12 minutes or until lightly browned

Date Bars

A good old fashioned date bar, from Grandma's kitchen

Mix	all ingredients in order as given below **1/2 cup melted butter** **2 eggs** **1/4 teaspoon baking powder** **1 cup walnuts,** chopped fine **1 cup sugar** **3/4 cup flour** **1/8 teaspoon salt** **1 cup chopped dates**
Spread	into greased 9 x 13 inch pan
Bake	at 350° for 20 minutes. Cool for 10 minutes
Cut	into squares while still warm and roll in confectioner's sugar

Chewy Brownies

This fabulous brownie recipe was given to me by Margaret Campos. The joy of this brownie is that it can be made in one saucepan. It is by far the very best I have ever tasted!

Melt	**2 sq. bitter chocolate** with **2 blocks butter** on low heat Remove from heat and
Add	**2 cups sugar**, mixing well
Add	**2 large eggs,** one at a time, stirring quickly
Fold in	**1 cup pastry flour** **1 teaspoon vanilla** **1 cup chopped nuts**
Bake	at 300° for 55 minutes, in a greased 6 x 9 pan Do not over bake
Turn	oven *off.* Leave pan in oven 5 minutes longer Remove pan immediately
Loosen	sides from pan immediately. Cool for 1 hour. Cut in squares. Store in tightly covered jar

Simple Sugar Cookies

These will really go, so double the recipe!

Cream	**1/2 cup Crisco** **1/2 cup butter** with **1 cup sugar**
Add	**1 egg,** whole and mix well
Add	**2 1/2 cups pastry flour** gradually **1 teaspoon almond extract**

Roll	in small balls, between palms and place 3 inches Apart on lightly greased cookie sheet
Take	flat bottomed glass, dip in dish of sugar and press on cookie. Do not press too thin as cookie will crumble when baked
Top	with **walnut half** (optional)
Bake	at 375° for 12 minutes or until lightly browned

Dropped Shortbread Cookie

This cookie has the richness and favor of real shortbread. It is more delicate in texture. Makes a nice Christmas package for the neighbors, as it keeps well in a tightly covered can.

Mix	**1 1/2 cup pastry flour** with **1 cup sifted powdered sugar**
Cut	**2 blocks butter** with pastry blender. Knead 5 minutes
Drop	by teaspoons on ungreased cookie sheet
Prick	top of cookie with fork dipped in flour
Bake	300° for 15 minutes or until light brown If you double the recipe, increase the butter only by one stick

Popo's Almond Cookie

This is a cookie that may disappear before it even gets to the cookie jar. Be sure to double up on this recipe!

Cream	**1 cup sugar** **1 1/2 cups Crisco**
Add	**3 cups pastry flour** **1/4 teaspoon baking soda** **1/2 teaspoon salt**

Mix	**1 teaspoon almond extract** **1 beaten egg** **1/2 cup finely chopped walnuts**
Shape	into round balls and flatten slightly
Dot	the center of the cookie with a small cork dipped in red food coloring
Bake	at 350° for 10-12 minutes or until lightly browned
Cool	few minutes before from pan

English Toffee Sheet Cookies

Amy Tomita makes the yummiest cookies. This one is great and very easy to make.

Cream	**1 cup butter** **1 cup sugar** until smooth
Add	**1 egg yolk** and mix thoroughly
Add	**2 cups flour** **1 teaspoon cinnamon** Using hands, mixing lightly and thoroughly
Spread	on greased cookie sheet and smooth surface
Beat	**1 egg white** slightly and brush on top
Sprinkle	**1 cup chopped pecans** or **walnuts** over top and Press in slightly
Bake	at 275° for 1 hour
Cut	in squares while hot Makes 6 dozen 1 inch cookies

Peanut Butter
Chocolate Chip Cookies

From the kitchen of Mary Lepine comes this wonderful cookie recipe. It became the children's favorite summer "pin money" venture.

Cream	**1 1/2 cups Crisco** **1/2 cup butter**
Add	**2 cups granulated sugar** **2 cups brown sugar.** Beat well
Add	**4 eggs whole** **2 teaspoons vanilla.** Beat well
Stir	in **2 cups peanut butter** (chunky style)
Stir	together **4 cups flour** **4 teaspoons baking soda** **1 teaspoon salt** Stir into creamed mixture
Add	**1 large package chocolate chips**
Drop	by teaspoons onto ungreased cookie sheet, Flatten with fork
Bake	at 350° oven for 12-15 minutes or until light brown
Cool	slightly on cookie sheet as cookies tend to break easily when hot

Quick Ginger Cookies

Mix	**2/3 cup safflower oil** **1 cup sugar** **1 egg** **2 Tablespoons molasses**

Sift	2 cups flour
	2 teaspoons baking soda
	1 teaspoon powdered ginger
	1 teaspoon cinnamon
	1/2 teaspoon salt
Roll	in ball and flatten with flat bottomed glass dipped in sugar
Bake	at 350° oven for 12-15 minutes

Christmas Gingerbread Boys

Bag gingerbread boys in plastic bags and tie them with ribbons to hang on the Christmas tree branches. Give them out to all the "children."

Mix	1/2 cup butter
	1 cup brown sugar
	Until blended
Add	2 teaspoons salt
	2 teaspoons baking soda
	1 teaspoon cinnamon
	1 teaspoon cloves
	1 teaspoon allspice
	1 teaspoon ginger
Add	1 1/2 cups light molasses
	2/3 cups water or apple cider
	6 1/2 cups unsifted all purpose flour
Roll	out on floured board
Cut	into gingerbread boys and place on cookie sheet
Bake	at 350 for 10-15 minutes until lightly brown
Cool	and frost with Decorator's Icing

Decorator's Icing

Mix   **1 cup powdered sugar**
                        Dash of salt
                        1/2 teaspoon vanilla

Add   **1/3 cup water**, add 1 teaspoon at a time
                        Until stiff enough to decorate

Pecan Nuggets

Great for Christmas treats!

Cut   **2 blocks butter into**
                        2 cups flour
                        1/4 teaspoon salt

Add   **2 teaspoons vanilla**
                        1 cup finely chopped pecans
                        4 Tablespoons sifted powdered sugar

Roll   into a ball. Pinch off small pieces and form into small balls

Place   on ungreased cookie sheet

Bake   at 375° 12-15 minutes

Cool   on wire rack for 10 minutes

Roll.   Carefully in sifted powdered sugar

Cool   Completely before storing in an air tight container

Easy Pie Crust

I came across this fabulous pie crust recipe 10 years ago. Not only is it the flakiest crust I have ever eaten, but the quickest and easiest to prepare. I use the vegetable oil because it is low in cholesterol.

Sift	**1 1/2 cup pastry flour** **1 1/2 teaspoon sugar** **1 teaspoon salt,** into ungreased pie pan
Combine	**1/2 cup vegetable oil** and **2 Tablespoons cold milk** in measuring cup
Whip	with fork until cloudy and pour over flour mixture Mix with fork until flour is blended
Shape	with hands pressing to pan shape (9 inch) Cover part of the rim and flute with fingers
Prick	and bake at 400° for 12-15 minutes

Willow's Coconut Cream Pie

The Willows' Coconut Cream Pie has always been a conversation piece. Not only is it beautiful to look at, but a delight to taste. Here it is!

Put	**2 cups milk** **1/2 cup sugar** **1/4 cup grated coconut** **Pinch of salt,** in a saucepan and let come to a near boil
Mix	**2 heaping Tablespoons cornstarch** **4 egg yolks together with a little water**
Add	to milk mixture, stirring continually Until thick (on a low fire)
Add	**1 Tablespoon butter** **vanilla to flavor**
Cool	and fill in pie shell. Top with meringue

Meringue

Beat	**4 egg whites** until stiff
Add	**1/4 teaspoon cream of tartar** **1/4 teaspoon salt**
Add	**1/2 cup sugar** slowly
Spread	over cooled filling, sealing to edges of pastry
Bake	in 350 for 15-20 minutes. Makes a 9 inch pie

Lemon Fluff Pie

Make this lemon fluff pie the night before. This pie will melt in your mouth.

Beat	**4 egg yolks** with **1/2 cup sugar** in the top of a double boiler until thick
Add	**juice of 3 lemons**
Cook	over hot water until slightly thick
Add	**grated rind of 3 lemons** and set aside to cool
Beat	**4 egg whites** with **1/8 teaspoons cream of tartar** until soft peaks are formed
Add	**1/2 cup sugar** gradually and beat until stiff
Fold	into egg yolk mixture
Pour	into **baked pie shell (9 inch)**
Bake	at 350° until lightly browned (12-15 minutes)
Remove	to rack and cool. Place in refrigerator overnight. Before serving spread top with whipped cream.

Green Mango Pie

You must use the very green mangoes for this pie. It will taste like a green apple pie, only better.

Pare	**6-8 large green mangoes** and cut into chunks (more if needed)
Place	in **9 inch unbaked pie shell**
Sprinkle	**1 1/4 cups white sugar** **Dot with butter** **2 Tablespoons lemon** or **lime juice** **1/2 teaspoon allspice** or **cinnamon**
Cover	with slitted top crust
Brush	top with cream mixed with a little sugar
Bake	at 400° for 15 minutes 350° for 40-45 minutes
Test	mangoes by pricking with fork to se if they are tender

Crumb Topping

Try this delicious crumb topping instead of the top pie crust for a delightful change.

Mix	**1 cup light brown sugar** **3/4 cup pastry flour**
Cut in	**1 block cold butter** until mixture is Crumbly and even in texture
Sprinkle	**1/2 cup finely chopped macadamia nuts** over crumb mixture. Bake as above

Best Custard Pie

Betty Ho contributed this wonderful Custard Pie. Betty says, "This makes a deep 10 inch pie, just right for company or a large family." It is so smooth and it tastes just as good as it looks!

Break	**5 large eggs** into a large bowl and Beat well with a fork
Add	**1 small can evaporated milk with fresh** **Milk to measure 4 cups**
Add	**1 teaspoon vanilla** **3/4 cup sugar less 2 level teaspoons** **1/2 teaspoon salt,** scant
Pour	into **unbaked pie shell**. To prevent spilling, Save 1 cup of custard to pour when pie is set in oven
Grate	**whole nutmeg** over the top of the pie
Bake	at 400° for 10 minutes 350° for 40 minutes Do not bake the pie too quickly or too long at it will water

Blueberries A La Mode

This yummy pie was donated by Mrs. John Diedrichs. Start with this unusual, flakey and delicious mayonnaise pie crust. Guaranteed to become a family favorite!

CRUST

Mix	**1/2 cup mayonnaise** **2 Tablespoons water**, add **1 1/2 cup flour**—mix well
Knead	and press into 9 inch pie pan. Bake at 425° for 12-15 minutes

FILLING

Whip	**1 cup unsweetened whip cream** until stiff. Set aside
Mix	**8 oz. cream cheese** with **3/4 cup sifted powdered sugar** in small bowl
Blend	with beaters until smooth and creamy
Fold	whipped cream into cream cheese mixture until just blended
Pour	into 9 inch baked pie shell
Spoon	one **1 lb. 5 ozs. can blueberry pie** filling over cream mixture Refrigerate until serving time

Bubby's Texas Pecan Pie

Smooth and delicious, this not too sweet" pecan pie is a perfect compliment to your Thanksgiving dinner. Be prepared to give away this recipe.

Beat	**3 large eggs**, slightly
Add	**1 cup sugar** **1 cup white Karo syrup** **1/4 teaspoon salt** **1 teaspoon vanilla** Mix well
Add	**1 1/2 cups broken pecan meats**
Place	in pastry lined 10 inch pan
Bake	450° for 10-15 minutes 350° for 35 minutes

Lemon Cake Pie

This unusual cake turns into a yummy pie. Not only for lemon lovers. Donated with love from Haralyn Schubert.

Cream	**1 cup sugar** **3 Tablespoons flour** **3 Tablespoons butter**
Separate	**2 large eggs**
Stir into	flour mixture **2 well beaten egg yolks**, slowly
Add	**juice and grated rind of 1 large lemon** **1/2 cup evaporated milk** diluted with **1/2 cup water** **1/4 teaspoon salt**
Beat	**Egg whites** in a separate bowl until stiff
Fold	beaten egg whites into creamed mixture
Pour	into a **9 inch, unbaked pie shell**
Bake	350° for 30 minutes or until firm

Passion Fruit Chiffon Pie

A light tangy pie, just right for hot summer days. Put this together in just fifteen minutes.

Soften	**1 Tablespoon unflavored gelatin in** **1/4 cup warm water**
Into a	medium saucepan put **5 medium egg yolks**, lightly beaten **2 Tablespoons sugar** **Juice of one large lemon** **1/2 teaspoon of grated lemon rind**
Cook	over medium heat, stirring constantly until thick Remove from heat

Add	softened gelatin to **1-6 oz. can thawed passion fruit nectar** Mix well. Set aside.
Whip	**5 egg whites until frothy and add 1/4 teaspoon salt.** Beat until stiff. Use a large bowl.
Slowly	fold the passion fruit mixture into the stiffly Beaten egg whites. DO NOT OVERBLEND.
Pour	into **9 inch, baked pie crust** and chill until serving time

Pineapple Cream Pie

Two minutes to prepare, smooth and delicious.

Combine	**1 large can drained crushed pineapple 1 large container whipped topping 3/4 cup chopped macadamia nuts 1/3 cup fresh lime juice 1 cup condensed milk 1 Tablespoon rum flavoring (opt)**
Divide	into **2 graham cracker crumb crusts**
Chill	2 hours before serving. Sprinkle **1/4 cup chopped macadamia nuts** over pie. May be frozen indefinitely and thawed out in the refrigerator for 4 hours.

Cheese Cake Supreme

Truly "out of this world" – light and high, it literally melts in your mouth.

Crush	**3/4 box Zwieback** into fine crumbs
Add	**1/2 cup powdered sugar** **1/2 cup melted butter**
Mix	well and press into a buttered 2 1/2 inch deep by 10 inch spring form pan. Cover bottom and sides. Use back of spoon for pressing. Reserve 1/4 cup of mixture for sprinkling. (opt)
Beat	**6 egg whites** at high speed until stiff but not dry. Set aside.
Beat	**6 egg yolks** until thick and creamy. Set aside.
Sift	**3 Tablespoons pastry flour** **1 1/2 cups sugar** **Pinch of salt** into a large bowl
Add	**16 ozs. Cream cheese** softened **1 teaspoon grated lemon rind** **1 Tablespoon lemon juice**. Blend well
Add	beaten egg yolk to flour mixture with **2 cups sour cream** at room temperature **1 teaspoon vanilla**, blend well
Fold	stiffly beaten egg whites into the mixture
Pour	into prepared pan. Sprinkle on remaining crumbs (opt)
Bake	300°-325° for 1 hour

Turn off heat. Prop door open slightly and cool for 1 hour.
Cheese cake will fall if there is a draft. It so, do not open oven door for 1 hour.

Fabulous Chocolate Cake

The utmost in chocolate cakes. A dark chocolate, with the yummiest flavor. A cake that tastes just as good two days later, if it lasts that long!

Melt	**3 squares chocolate** and cool
Cream	1 1/4 block butter with 1 package light brown sugar 2 large eggs, until well blended and light in color
Add	melted chocolate to batter with **2 teaspoon vanilla**. Mix well
Add	**2 1/4 cups cake flour** sifted with **1 teaspoon salt** (scant) and
Alternate	**1/2 cup buttermilk** with flour
Mix	**2 teaspoons baking soda** in **1 cup boiling water** and add last to batter. Stir quickly
Pour	into 2 or 3 greased, waxed lined 8 inch round or square pans
Bake	360° for 10 minutes, then lower to 350° for 25 minutes for 3 layers 30-35 minutes for 2 layers.

Chocolate Pudding Frosting

A pudding frosting that holds its shape and will not absorb into the cake.

Cook	**1 1/2 cup granulated sugar** **1/4 teaspoon salt** **1 1/2 cups hot water** **2 squares chocolate** over low heat until chocolate is melted
Mix	**7 Tablespoons cornstarch** gradually into **4 Tablespoons evaporated milk** Add to chocolate and stir continuously

| Cook | until mixture thickens, on medium heat (15 minutes) |
| | Stir rapidly as mixture comes to a boil |

Remove	from heat and add
	1 teaspoon vanilla
	1 Tablespoon butter

| Cool | frost 2 or 3 layers of chocolate cake |

| Sprinkle | top of cake **with chopped walnuts, pecans** |
| | **or macadamia nuts** |

Heaven Sent Banana Cake

Auntie Grace's heavenly banana cake is a moist cake with an old fashioned flavor. A treasured family secret shared by Peggy D. Andrews. Put a star next to this recipe!

| Cream | **1 cup butter** with |
| | **2 cups sugar** |

| Add | **4 eggs**, one at a time, beating well after each addition |

Alternate	**4 cups sifted flour** mixed with
	2 teaspoons baking soda
	6 medium sized mashed bananas

| Stir in | **1 cup chopped walnuts** or **pecans** |
| | **12 oz. package chocolate chips** |

| Pour | into 9 x 11 pan, lightly oiled and floured |

| Bake | 350° for 45 minutes |

| Cool | thoroughly (3hours) before frosting. |
| | VERY IMPORTANT! |

"Angel" Flour Frosting

Auntie Grace's unusual flour frosting. Light as a feather and so yummy. This is a bowl licker!

Stir	**6 Tablespoons flour** in **1 cup milk** in a small saucepan
Cook	over medium heat, stirring until thickens into Paste like consistency. Remove from heat and cool.
Cream	**1 cup butter** **1 cup sugar** until fluffy
Add	flour paste to creamed mixture, stirring until well blended
Add	**1 teaspoon vanilla.** Mix well

Fruit Cocktail Cake

Joyce's "Happy Cake". The very best fruit cocktail cake, moist and delicious.

Beat	together **1 1/2 cup sugar** **2 eggs**
Add	**2 cups fruit cocktail** (partially drained)
Sift	together **2 cups flour** **2 teaspoons baking soda** **1/4 teaspoon salt.** Sift into first mixture
Add	**1 teaspoon vanilla.** Mix well. Pour into 13 x 9 x 2 pan greased and floured
Sprinkle	with **1 cup chopped nuts** **1-2 cups coconut** **1 cup brown sugar** Bake at 350° for 45 minutes

Stir	**3/4 cup sugar** **1/2 cup evaporated milk** **1 stick butter**, in a small saucepan
Bring	to boil. Cook for 3 minutes
Pour	over hot cake

Date Chocolate Chip Cake

Another of Dora's favorites. This moist flavorful cake doesn't need to be frosted – great to take on picnics.

Grease	a 9 x13 inch pan. Flour with cocoa and shake out excess
Pour	**1 1/4 cup boiling water** over **1 box chopped, pitted dates**. Cool
Cream	**1 1/2 block butter** with **1 cup sugar**
Add	**2 large eggs**, beat well
Sift	**2 cups all purpose flour with** **1 teaspoon baking soda** **1/2 teaspoon salt** **1 Tablespoon Nestles Quick cocoa**
Add	flour to shortening mixture Alternating with date mixture
Add	dry ingredients first and last. Pour batter into pan
Sprinkle	over batter **1/4 cup sugar** **1/2 cup chopped walnuts** **6 oz. package semi-sweet chocolate chips**
Bake	at 350° for 30-35 minutes

Easy Mocha Frosting

Melt	**4 1/2 squares of unsweetened chocolate** over hot water Cool
Blend	together **3 1/2 cups confectioners' sugar** **6 Tablespoons soft butter**
Add	**1 1/2 Tablespoons evaporated milk** **1/4 cup instant coffee** (prepared with water) **1 1/2 teaspoons vanilla** **1/4 teaspoon salt** Beat until well blended
Beat	**2 eggs** into coffee mixture
Blend	in cooled chocolate. If frosting is too soft add a little more confectioners' sugar.

If you like strong coffee flavor, prepare to your taste

Jello Cream Crunch

A layered dessert with a delicious macadamia nut shortbread crust. Best done overnight.

Cream	**1 1/2 block butter** **1/3 cup brown sugar** **1/2 cup chopped macadamia nuts** **1 1/2 cup flour**
Press	into 9 x 13 pan
Bake	at 350° for 10 minutes or until lightly brown. Cool
Mix	**1 large box black cherry jello** (6 oz.) With **3 cups hot water** – set aside to cool

Cream	**8 oz. cream cheese**
	3/4 cup sifted powdered sugar
Fold in	**1 cup whipped, whipping cream**
Spoon	into cooled crust sealing edges well
	Set in refrigerator for 20-30 minutes
Spoon	cooled jello over cream cheese mixture
	Set in refrigerator until firm
Cut	into squares, decorate with whipped cream and serve

Fritz's Buttermilk Pound Cake

This is my husband's favorite cake. Try it; it may be your favorite too!

Combine	in a large bowl;
	4 eggs
	1/2 lb. butter
	2 cups sugar
	1 teaspoon vanilla
	1 teaspoon lemon extract (optional) or
	Juice of 1/2 lemon
	Beat at high speed until fluffy, lemony and very light
Sift	**3 cups sifted flour**
	1/2 teaspoon baking soda
	1/2 teaspoon baking powder
	1/4 teaspoon salt
Alternate	**1 cup buttermilk** with dry ingredients
Grease	2 loaf pans and line with was paper
Pour	batter into pans
Bake	55-60 minutes, 325° oven

107

Orange Butter Sponge Cake

Moist, light, feathery, comes this contribution from the "Garden Isle" of Kauai. Superb!

Beat	1/2 hour on high speed **7 eggs** **1 1/2 cups sugar**
Squeeze	**3/4 cup orange juice** (approximately 2 medium oranges) Set aside
Melt	**1 block butter,** set aside
Sift	together **1 1/2 cup cake flour** **1 3/4 teaspoon baking powder** (double action)
Fold	flour into egg mixture quickly. Blending well
Dribble in	**3/4 cup orange juice** **1 blk. Cooled, melted butter** *Very slowly* into mixture
Mix	thoroughly. This is VERY IMPORTANT. DO NOT OVER BEAT!
Put	into ungreased 10 inch sponge cake pan
Bake	at 325° for 50-55 minutes, on lowest oven rack
Cool	cake inverted on a funnel

Hawaiian Delight

Not too sweet – perfect as a light dessert and can be made one day ahead. You must try it!

Bake	**1 yellow cake mix** as directed in a 13 x 9 inch pan
Cool	completely

Mix	**6 ozs. Jello instant vanilla pudding** In blender, prepare as directed
Add	**8 ozs. Softened cream cheese** to pudding and blend well
Spread	over cooled cake
Drain	**1 large can unsweetened crushed pineapple** well and spoon over pudding
Spread	1 large container whipped topping over pineapple
Sprinkle	**1 cup finely chopped macadamia nuts** Over whipped topping, chill well for 1 hour

Delicious White Frosting

This fluffy white frosting that swirls into any design was given to me by Mary Lepine. Mary always has some new and wonderful recipes to share.

Boil	without stirring! **1/2 cup water** **1 cup sugar** **1 teaspoon white vinegar** **1/4 teaspoon cream of tartar** until mixture forms a thin thread when dripped from a spoon. (approx. 15 minutes)
Beat	**egg whites** – when frothy add **1/4 teaspoon salt**. Beat until stiff. Pour syrup slowly into egg white mixture. Beating with electric beaters at medium speed. Scrape sides with spatula and continue beating until mixture is thick and slightly cooled.
Add	**1 teaspoon vanilla** to frosting

Peach Surprise

If you are wondering just what to do with those old crusts of bread, this is your answer. The bread bakes to a crunchy crust topping and children love it.

Beat	**3 eggs** **3/4 cup sugar** **1 teaspoon cinnamon** until very light and fluffy
Add	**2 cups shredded bread** and fold into egg mixture
Place	**cling peach halves or slices** in the bottom of baking dish. Keep the juice for punch to go with the dessert
Spoon	bread mixture over the peaches
Bake	at 400° for 20-25 minutes
	*the next time you bake bread pudding try adding 1 heaping tablespoon of orange marmalade or pineapple-papaya jam to your bread pudding mixture

Almond Float

A light dessert, a perfect compliment to an oriental meal. Perfected by Anna Stewart, and generously passed on for your enjoyment.

Soften	**3 packages of unflavored gelatin** in **1/2 cup water**
Scald	**2 3/4 cup water** **1 1/2 can evaporated milk** **1 cup sugar**, stir frequently
Add	softened gelatin. Cool
Add	**3 teaspoons almond extract**
Pour	into 9 x 13 pan. Refrigerate 4 hours or preferably overnight

Cube	almond gelatin and place in a serving bowl
Add	**1 can fruit cocktail** **1 can mandarin oranges** **1 can lychees**

Italian Strawberry Meringue

Our most successful party dessert. Never fails to bring compliments!

Beat	**8-10 large egg whites** until stiff
Add	**pinch of salt**. Continue beating
Add	**1 cup sugar and** **1/4 teaspoon cream of tartar** gradually Continue beating
Add	**1 Tablespoon white vinegar** **1 teaspoon vanilla.** Continue beating
Spoon	into 2 wax lined round pans and smooth
Place	pans over water
Bake	in 250° oven for 45 minutes Cool slowly in oven. Before serving
Whip	**1 cup whipping cream**. Slide one layer of meringue onto serving dish. Spread 1/2 cup whipped cream on layer
Spoon	layer of **sugared drained strawberries** over cream and top with second layer
Place	remaining cream on second layer and Dot with remaining strawberries
	*If you use frozen strawberries, do not thaw out completely as the berries will tend to be mushy.

Instant Coffee Rum Cake

This luscious dessert will take care of the egg yolk problem. You will need **3 dozen lady fingers** for the cake part of this recipe.

Cream	**1 lb. butter** until soft
Add	**6 egg yolks** **2 cups powdered sugar** **2 jiggers rum** **1 teaspoon vanilla** **2 Tablespoons instant coffee** in 2 Tablespoons hot water
Beat	all ingredients well
Place	in tubeless angel food pan with removable bottom
Alternate	lady fingers with batter, ending with lady fingers
Leave	part of creamed mixture for frosting
Refrigerate	2 or more hours. Lift from pan, keeping cake on the bottom portion of pan
Frost	with leftover creamed mixture and top with **toasted almonds**
Toast	**almonds** in 1 Tablespoon butter until light brown, in 350° oven

Mocha Mint Mousse

So simple, so elegant - a quick last minute dessert just because "you" are so special

Separate	**4 large eggs** (room temperature)
Beat	**egg whites** in small bowl till stiff but not dry. Set aside
Whirl	**6 ozs. Semi- sweet chocolate pieces** in blender into bits
Add	**1/4 cup boiling coffee**
Add	**2 teaspoons vanilla** **1/2 teaspoons mint flavoring** or **1 Tablespoon crème de menthe liqueur** **4 egg yolks,** blend for 1 minute
Add	swiftly into the chocolate mixture **1 cup whipped whipping crème** **1 cup cool whip**
Fold	chocolate mixture into beaten egg whites until no egg white shows
Spoon	into long stemmed glasses and chill

Hot Fudge Sauce

Liliann's smooth, thick, absolutely yummy fudge sauce is a teenager's delight. A quick last minute treat. Delicious spooned over all ice cream flavors. My favorite is Kona coffee ice cream, layered with sauce, topped with whipped cream, garnished with chopped macadamia nuts and a cherry!

Melt	**1 large package chocolate chips** **1/2 cup package large marshmallows** **1/2 cup milk** in top of a double boiler
Stir	with spatula until smooth More milk may be added to thin sauce

Café Lolo

Bill Mullahey, connoisseur of fine liqueurs, offered this wonderful after-dinner coffee. Definitely smooth with a nut-like flavor, it will be long remembered.

Brew   **coffee** to taste

Into   **1 cup of hot black coffee**

Add   **1 jigger Tia Maria liqueur** or your favorite coffee liqueur

Float   **2 teaspoons *coconut cream** on top

*To make coconut cream, grate fresh coconut into cheesecloth. Wring juice out of the coconut meat. It will refrigerate into a cream cheese consistency. Or, tear carton off frozen coconut milk. Scrape clear liquid off bottom of frozen milk. Put remainder into double boiler and cook over boiling water to evaporate excess liquid. Cook until cream is quite thick. Refrigerate until ready for use. Lolo may now be purchased at the supermarket.

Lolo – Fijian word for coconut cream.

Recipes For Health

Dedicated

to my children

CHRIS, CELIA, TIM, BECKY, MARI, GREG
and their families

BUBBY,
a special friend

and

ANNETTE, BARBARA, CATHARINE, ROSALIE, & VICTOR

Preface

Ten years ago, I and a few special friends, opened LIVING FOODS, a complete health food and nutritional center in the heart of Kaneohe. Our purpose was to share knowledge of health and nutrition with the community. We presented educational seminars, cooking classes, tours for school children and an awareness of a healthy life-style for all age groups. Out of the LIVING FOODS kitchen came the much requested recipes, some of which are presented ion this portion of the cookbook.

To further enhance a concept of healthy living, I would like to share what I have found to be the first step towards health, DETOXIFICATION: a natural cleansing of the body's elimination system. With the ever-increasing awareness of additives, chemicals and preservatives in our food and the abundance of toxic wastes in our environment, the need for preventative health measures becomes inevitable. One of the very best detoxification programs available today is the **Beneficial Health and Nutrition** 3-day all-natural detoxification program.

For further information, write to me at:

> Better Health Unlimited
> Post Office Box 1592
> Kaneohe, Hawaii 96744

Detoxifying 3-4 times a year will help to keep you in optimum health, keep your weight under control, and help to retard the aging process through proper elimination.

Selecting foods from the new health section may become for you and your family a new adventure in healthy eating. ENJOY!

Laurie Bachran

*all ingredients in this section are available in health food stores or in the health food section of your grocery store.

116

Pupus

Chili Con Quesas

Be sure to double this recipe. If there are leftovers, it can be reheated. This zesty hot dip should be served with tortilla chips.

Sauté	In a medium saucepan **1 large diced onion** **4 cloves minced garlic in** **2 Tablespoons safflower oil** until grazed
Add	**4 Tablespoons whole wheat flour** **5 oz. can evaporated milk**
Stir	until ingredients form a thick paste
Add	**2 cans roasted peeled, green chilies,** seeded and diced **2 cans (#2) stewed, sliced tomatoes**
Add	**1/2 lb. grated Monterey Jack cheese** **1 small jar diced tomatoes** **Salt** to taste
Pour	into serving bowl to serve

Super Mex Layered Dip

This scrumptious dip will serve a dozen or more guests!

Combine	**3 medium ripe avocados,** mashed **2 Tablespoons fresh lemon juice** **1/2 teaspoon vege-sal** **1/4 teaspoon cayenne.** Set aside
Combine	**1 cup light sour cream** **1/2 cup light mayonnaise** **1 package Taco mix.** Set aside
Combine	**4 cups refried beans** (see Bean Tostada recipe) **2 Tablespoons diced jalapeno peppers (hot)**
Prepare	**1 cup chopped green onions** **3 medium tomatoes,** seeded and diced **Two 3 1/2 ounce cans pitted ripe black olives,** chopped **8 oz. grated sharp cheddar cheese**
Spread	bean mixture in a large oblong glass dish
Layer	in order with Avocado mixture Sour cream mixture Chopped green onions Diced tomatoes Chopped black olives Grated cheddar cheese
Serve	at room temperature with **tortilla chips**. OLE! Chill if prepared ahead in the refrigerator.

Guacamole

Cut	**4 large ripe avocados** into small cubes with a silver knife
Squeeze	**juice of 1/2 lemon** over pears
Mix	**4 Tablespoons olive oil, 1 medium onion,** finely minced, **2 teaspoons salt, 1 small bunch of "Chinese parsley",** finely minced. Mix well and serve with chips
	*1/2 handful of dried coriander or 1 small bunch of regular parsley may be substituted for the chinese parsley.

Lemon Herbed Marinated Mushrooms

Put into	quart size mayonnaise jar **1/2 cup cold pressed oil** **3 Tablespoons lemon** or **lime juice** **1 Tablespoon stone ground prepared mustard** **1/2 teaspoon vege-sal** **Dash of cayenne pepper** **1 Tablespoon minced parsley.** Shake well
Slice	**2 or more (to fill jar) cups mushrooms** sliced 1/8 inch thick. Shake gently. Marinate at room temperature for an hour. Store in refrigerator.

Spinach Dip

Thaw	and drain **1 package chopped frozen spinach**
Combine	With **1/3 cup chopped green onions** (scallions) **1/2 cup plain yogurt** **1/2 cup cold-processed mayonnaise** **1/2 teaspoon vege-sal** **1/4 teaspoon dill weed** Blend and let stand for 1 hour
Serve	with **corn chips** or **toasted pita bread triangles**

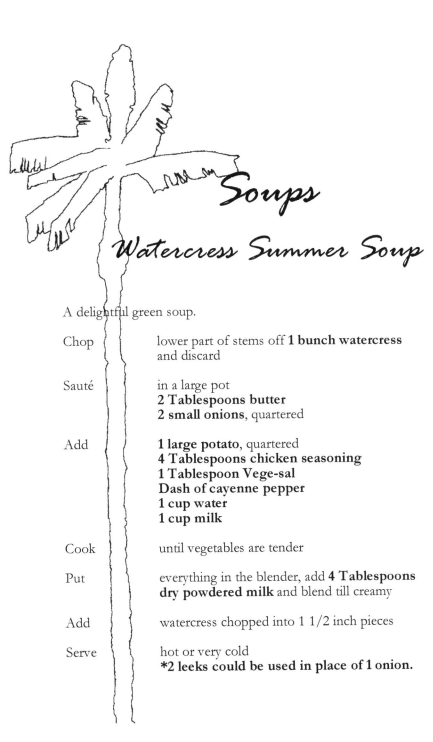

Soups

Watercress Summer Soup

A delightful green soup.

Chop	lower part of stems off **1 bunch watercress** and discard
Sauté	in a large pot **2 Tablespoons butter** **2 small onions**, quartered
Add	**1 large potato**, quartered **4 Tablespoons chicken seasoning** **1 Tablespoon Vege-sal** **Dash of cayenne pepper** **1 cup water** **1 cup milk**
Cook	until vegetables are tender
Put	everything in the blender, add **4 Tablespoons dry powdered milk** and blend till creamy
Add	watercress chopped into 1 1/2 inch pieces
Serve	hot or very cold ***2 leeks could be used in place of 1 onion.**

French Onion Soup

Simple version of this traditional French soup

Melt	in large pot **1 block unsalted butter**
Slice	**8 medium onions** and sauté in butter
Add	**2 rounded Tablespoons whole wheat flour** And stir until blended
Mix	together in large bowl **8 cups of water** **8 teaspoons vegetable protein seasoning** **1 Tablespoon vege-sal** Add to onions and cook for 30 minutes
Serve	in bowl with **square toast** topped **with grated jack cheese**

Cream of Potato Soup

The blender whips this recipe into a thick creamy soup.

Sauté	in pan **2 Tablespoons butter** **1 very large onion,** quartered **2 cloves garlic**
Add	**4-5 large potatoes,** peeled and cut in quarters **12 cups water** **1 Tablespoon dill weed** **4 Tablespoons vegetable protein seasoning** **2 Tablespoons vege-sal** **2 Tablespoons Bragg Liquid Aminos** **1 stalk celery** **1/4 green bell pepper, chopped** **Dash of cayenne pepper**
Cook	all together till tender

Blend	till smooth in blender adding 3 ozs. of powdered milk with each blender full of potato mixture
	Serve with chopped chives or finely chopped parsley

Greek Style Lentil Soup

A hearty soup for cool days. A recipe from my Greek friend Eleni's kitchen.

Soak	**2 cups lentils** after cleaning and rinsing well. 1-2 hours
Saute	in **4-5 Tablespoons olive oil** **1 small onion**, chopped **3-4 garlic cloves**, chopped
Into	a large pot put **8 cups of water** Soaked lentils and sautéed vegetables **3-4 carrots,** cut in cubes
Simmer	1 1/2 hours or until lentils are cooked. Season to taste

Eggplant Barley Soup

The most requested soup for the Living Foods Kitchen, created by Annette Rinell, chef par excellence.

Sauté in	**4 Tablespoons oil** until golden brown **2 large onions** chopped **2 cloves garlic** minced
Add	**12 cups water** **2 Tablespoons basil** **3 Tablespoons Bragg Liquid Aminos** **3 Tablespoons vege-sal** **5 Tablespoons beef seasoning** **Dash of cayenne pepper** **5-6 long eggplants,** sliced 1/2 inch thick OR **2 rounded eggplants**, cubed **1 cup barley**, washed
Cook	in pressure cooker at 15 lbs., for six minutes

Jeanette's Gazpacho

Jeanette Parry from West Palm Beach, Florida, a warm and gracious hostess, shares her recipe to highlight that special luncheon on a hot summer's day. Jeanette has added extra zip to make this dish a memorable one!

Wash	**6 large ripe tomatoes**, core and coarsely chop. Save the juice
Wash	**2 sweet red peppers** **2 large cucumbers** Core, seed and coarsely chop
Chop	**2 leeks in large pieces** **2 large shallots**
Drop	in running food processor **1 clove garlic,** peeled **4 Tablespoons fresh parsley**
Add	tomatoes, peppers, cucumbers, leeks, shallots
Add	**1/2 cup olive oil** **1 1/2 cups v-8 juice** **1 cup Spicy v-8 juice.** Process only Until vegetables are chopped fine, but not pureed.
Put	into a large container with cover, add juice from tomatoes
Season	with **1/2 cup red wine vinegar, salt and pepper** to taste
Refrigerate	4 hours or overnight May be thinned with more v-8 juice
Serve	with **crispy croutons, diced cucumbers, tomatoes, leeks, and peppers. ENJOY!**

Salads

Spinach Salad Oriental

A very different spinach salad. Guaranteed to please the most discriminating.

Combine
1 bunch Horenso spinach, tear into bite size pieces
10-12 sliced water chestnuts
10-12 sliced mushrooms
1 bag of bean sprouts
1 large Kula onion, sliced
1 teaspoon unhulled sesame seeds

Toss
with **Tamari Dressing** and serve immediately

Tamari Seed Dressing

Tamari is a natural shoyu sauce.

Whiz
in blender
Scant 2/3 cup Tamari
3 Tablespoons fresh lime juice
1 teaspoon honey
1 teaspoon toasted sesame seeds
1 teaspoon chopped onions
Blend well

Add
1/4 cup safflower oil slowly
to tamari mixture until well blended

Special Cole Slaw

Slice   **1/2 head cabbage,** very fine

Add   **2-3 apples** sliced in thin sections

Add   **2 Tablespoons plain yogurt**
                   Mayonnaise, enough to moisten
                   1/2 cup raisins
                   1/2 cup sunflower seeds

Serve   CHILLED!

Broccoli Salad

Mary Delpech of Miami, Florida sends this unique salad. Not only delicious but full of fiber.

Mix   together in a large bowl
                   1 head broccoli, diced
                   1 head cauliflower, diced
                   1 red onion, diced
                   10 slices low-fat bacon fried crisp and diced*
                   1/2 cup raisins

Mix   **1 cup light mayonnaise***
                   2-3 Tablespoons honey
                   2 Tablespoons cider vinegar

Pour   mayonnaise mixture over vegetables

Marinate   2 hours or longer in refrigerator

                   *soy bacon bits may be used
                   *Ranch dressing packet mixed with yogurt can be substituted

Mai Fun
(Chinese Rice Stick Salad)

This wonderful colorful salad can be served as an entrée. A real crowd pleaser!

Chop	**1/2 cup peanuts**, set aside
Slice	**2 cups cooked chicken breasts** into julienne strips, set aside
Mix	in large bowl **1/2 teaspoon sugar** **1/2 teaspoon sesame oil** **1/2 teaspoon salt** **Dash of white pepper** **2 teaspoons oyster sauce** **2 teaspoons oyster sauce** **2 teaspoons soy sauce** **2 teaspoons salad oil** **2 teaspoons sherry or rice wine** **2 Tablespoons red Chinese vinegar** Marinate chicken in sauce for 30 minutes
Mix	in large bowl **2 cups head lettuce**, thinly sliced **2 cups won bok** (Chinese white cabbage), finely sliced **1 cup green onions**, sliced in 1 1/2 inch lengths **1 bunch chinese parsley (cilantro)**, chopped **1 cup celery**, finely sliced **1 large red bell pepper**, seeded, thinly sliced
In	**1 cup hot oil**, deep fry **1/2 package rice sticks (mai fun)** drain on paper towels
Mix	together just before serving
Toss	with half fried mai fun. and half of chopped peanuts. Mix well
Put	on serving platter and top with remaining mai fun and chopped peanuts

Creamy Herb Dressing

Combine in blender
1/4 cup safflower oil
1/4 cup apple cider vinegar
1 Tablespoon lemon or lime juice
1 cup cottage cheese
3/4 cup milk
1/2 teaspoon vege-sal
1/2 teaspoon Spike
1 bunch parsley
1 teaspoon basil
1 teaspoon tarragon
1 teaspoon rosemary
1/2 teaspoon celery seed

Makes 2 cups

Herb Salad Dressing

Use over salad greens—romaine, red cabbage, alfalfa sprouts, tomatoes, cucumbers, mushrooms and sunflower seeds.

In blender
1 1/4 cup safflower oil
1 1/4 cup lemon juice
2 1/2 teaspoon sea salt
1/4 teaspoon thyme leaves
1/4 teaspoon rosemary leaves
1/8 teaspoon sage leaves
1 bunch parsley
1/2 cup and 2 Tablespoons raw honey
1/4 cup water

Blend together. Refrigerate in a quart jar.

Green Goddess with Tofu

Whiz   in blender
8 ozs. tofu
1 cup buttermilk
2 Tablespoons Parmesan cheese
1 clove garlic
1/4 cup fresh parsley leaves
2 Tablespoons chopped onions
1/2 teaspoon sea salt
2 Tablespoons vinegar
1 teaspoon dry mustard
1 Tablespoon honey
On high speed until smooth and parsley has colored dressing green.

Chill   to blend flavors. Cover tightly and refrigerate.

Honey Salad Dressing

Place   in order in a quart jar
1 teaspoon paprika
1/2 teaspoon dry mustard
1/2 teaspoon salt
1/2 cup honey
3 Tablespoons lemon juice
1/4 cup apple cider vinegar
1 Tablespoon grated onion
1 cup safflower oil
1/2 teaspoon celery salt.

Shake   well. Excellent on fruit.

Yogurt Orange Dressing

Toss fresh cubed fruit with this refreshing yogurt dressing.

Mix   together
1 cup plain yogurt
1/4 cup frozen orange concentrate

One Jar Caesar Salad Dressing

Into   pint jar, put
4 Tablespoons lemon juice
1/4 cup olive oil
1/2 teaspoon freshly ground pepper
1 teaspoon Worcestershire
1/2 teaspoon garlic powder
1/2 teaspoon salt
1 egg beaten
1/2 cup parmesan cheese
1 teaspoon minced fresh coriander (Chinese parsley)

Shake   and refrigerate

Serve   over **romaine lettuce with bacon bits and fresh croutons**

Sesame Dressing

Whiz   in blender
1 teaspoon lecithin
1/2 cup sesame oil
1/2 cup soy or safflower oil
1/4 cup lemon juice
1/4 cup apple cider or wine vinegar
1 teaspoon sea salt or celery salt
1 tablespoon honey
1/2 teaspoon oregano or fine herbs
1/2 teaspoon paprika
1/8 teaspoon cayenne pepper
2 cloves garlic
1/4 cup sesame seeds

Refrigerate   Makes 1 pint.

Entrees

Ratatouille

Absolutely wonderful over baked potatoes, topped with creamed cottage cheese mixture.

Sauté in	**2 Tablespoons all blend oil** **2 zucchini** cut lengthwise then in 1/4 inch slices **3 cloves chopped garlic** in a large frying pan
Add	**1 onion** cut into wedges **1 large eggplant**, cut into small squares (opt) **1 large tomato** in wedges **1/2 pound of sliced fresh mushrooms** **1 teaspoon vege-sal** **2 Tablespoons Bragg Liquid Aminos** **Dash of cayenne pepper**
Cover	and cook approximately for 15 minutes DO NOT OVERCOOK
	TOPPING:
Blend	**1 cup cottage cheese**, in blender
Add	**1 teaspoon thyme** **2-3 Tablespoons milk** **Blend until smooth**
Serve	ratatouille over **baked potato.** **Brown rice or noodles** will work too!
Top	with a generous spoonful of **cottage cheese mixture,** **low Fat yogurt or light sour cream**

Spicy Indian Vegetarian Stew

A delicious variation. Wonderful with brown rice and yogurt! Created with Annette's special touch.

Sauté	in **1/4 cup oil** **1 lb. yellow turnips** peeled and cut in 1 inch cubes **2 large potatoes** peeled and cubed In a large pot for 10 minutes or until light brown
Add	**3 medium onions**, chopped coarse, cook until tender
Mix	in a bowl **3 cloves garlic**, minced **1 teaspoon cumin** **1/2 teaspoon fresh grated ginger** **1/2 teaspoon red pepper flakes** OR **2 small red chili peppers** mashed to form a paste.
Push	vegetables to one side of pan. Add garlic paste to the clear side of pan. Cook and stir for 3 minutes
Add	**2 cups water** **3 medium tomatoes**, chopped **1 teaspoon sea salt**
Stir	to mix pan ingredients. Cover
Simmer	stirring occasionally for 40 minutes or until vegetables are barely tender
Add	**1 cup frozen peas** **1 cup fresh green beans** cut in 2 inch pieces Cover
Simmer	stirring often for 20 minutes or until vegetables are barely tender and most liquid is absorbed
Sprinkle	with **parsley** before serving

Serve   with cooked brown rice and yogurt

Tofu Mushroom Loaf

A **"Living Foods"** favorite. Serve with brown rice and a green salad.

Sauté in   **2 Tablespoons oil**
                  1/2 onion, chopped
                  2 cloves garlic chopped
                  1 cup fresh mushrooms, sliced

Combine   in a large bowl, the above 4 items together with
                  1 block tofu, crumbled (squeeze tofu in paper towels
                  To remove excess water)
                  1/4 cup green onions, chopped
                  1/4 cups carrots, grated
                  1 teaspoon vege-sal
                  2 Tablespoons Bragg Liquid Aminos
                  2 Tablespoons safflower oil
                  2 eggs, slightly beaten
                  1 cup whole wheat bread crumbs, dash of cayenne

Place   in a loaf pan

Top   with grated **Jack cheese**

Bake   at 350° for 30 minutes, or until cheese is melted and
                  golden brown

Tofu Mushroom Burger

Serve on whole wheat buns with sprouts, sliced tomatoes, and cucumber.
Even the kids love it!

Sauté in   **2 Tablespoons safflower oil** until golden
                  1 onion chopped
                  2 large cloves garlic minced

Place   in bowl

Add	**1 cup whole wheat bread crumbs**
Add	**1 block Tofu**, drained well and mashed **1 Tablespoon Bragg Liquid Aminos** **Dash of cayenne pepper** **1 Tablespoon vege-sal** **1 egg**, beaten **2 Tablespoons Wheat Germ** (opt) **2 Tablespoons minced parsley**
Form	into patties and fry

Tofu Goes Italian

An easy to prepare casserole. Make ahead and refrigerate. Pop into the oven when guests arrive and serve in squares.

Cook	in boiling water. **3/4 package of vegeroni noodles** till tender DO NOT OVERCOOK. Drain water and set aside
Mix	in a blender until smooth **1 block Tofu** **3 eggs** **1 can (8oz.) tomato sauce** **2-4 cloves garlic** **2 teaspoons basil** **1 teaspoon oregano** **1 teaspoon vege-sal** **2 Tablespoons onion powder** **Dash of cayenne pepper** **2-4 Tablespoons grated parmesan cheese**
Add	**2 Tablespoons flour** and blend again
Fold	into the blended mixture **1 bell pepper**, finely chopped **1 cup chopped green onion** **1/2 cup chopped ripe olives** **2 Tablespoons chopped pimentos**

Mix	in well with the cooked noodles
Turn	half the tofu noodle mixture into an oiled 2 quart casserole
Cover	with a thinly sliced layer of **Mozzarella cheese (8oz.)** Save half of the cheese slices
Spread	the remaining noodles and tofu mixture over the cheese slices
Top	with remaining cheese slices
Bake	at 350° for 50-60 minutes or until golden brown

Tofu Parisienne

A **FIVE** minute dinner. It has the flavor of "**escargots**."
Love the garlic!

Sauté in	a wok or a large frying pan **4 Tablespoons unsalted butter** **2 large cloves chopped garlic** **1/2 lb. sliced fresh mushrooms** until glazed
Add	**1 teaspoon oregano** **1 small bunch chopped parsley** **1/2 teaspoon vege-sal** **1/4 cup Tamari** **1 block tofu** cut into small cubes
Toss	over medium heat until well coated
Serve	over **cooked brown rice**

Tofu Vegetarian Chili

The longer it cooks, the better the flavor.

Sauté	in **2 Tablespoons of oil** **1 small clove crushed garlic** **1 cup chopped onions** **1 cup chopped green peppers** **1 cup chopped celery** **2 1/2 cups crushed tomatoes** until soft, adding water as needed
Crumble	**1 block of hard tofu** in a bowl
Add	**1/8 packet chili spice mix** (any brand) **1/4 teaspoon cumin** **1/4 teaspoon celery seed** **Dash of cayenne pepper** Marinate tofu/spice mixture for 1/2 hour then
Add	to cooked vegetables, continue cooking on low heat
Add	**2 cups of cooked kidney beans**
Cook	for at least one hour.
Serve	in a ring of **cooked brown rice**

Tofu Puff Balls

Mix	together **1 block tofu**—drained and crumbled **1/4 cup minced green onions** **1/4 cups grated carrots** **One 8oz. can water chestnuts**, drained and chopped **6 medium size mushrooms**, minced **1 teaspoon vege-sal** **1 Tablespoon Tamari** **1 Tablespoon Bragg Liquid Aminos** **1/2 teaspoon grated ginger** **1/4 teaspoon dry mustard**

2 eggs, slightly beaten

Form	into walnut size balls and
Sauté	in **1 Tablespoon peanut oil**
Turning	carefully to brown all sides

Pineapple Sesame Sauce

Mix	in a saucepan

Juice from 5 oz. can unsweetened pineapple chunks
4 Tablespoons apple cider vinegar
2 1/2 Tablespoons sugar
1 teaspoon arrowroot
1 Tablespoon unhulled sesame seeds
Dash of cayenne pepper

Bring	to a boil and simmer until clear
Add	**pineapple chunks**
Serve	over Tofu Puffs

High Protein Loaf

A nutritious, delicious loaf. You will not miss the meat!

Mix well	in large bowl

2 cups cottage cheese
1 cup chopped walnuts
1 package onion soup mix (any brand)
3 medium eggs
4 Tablespoons safflower oil
1 teaspoon poultry seasoning
2 Tablespoons Bragg Liquid Aminos
3 cups wheat cereal flakes

Pour into	loaf pan and bake at 350° for 30 minutes or until nicely browned

Onion Mushroom Gravy

Sauté in	**2 Tablespoons unsalted butter** **1/2 of large onion** thinly sliced till glazed **1 1/2 cups sliced fresh mushrooms**
Add	stir in bowl **2 slightly rounded teaspoons arrowroot flour** **2 teaspoons vegetable protein seasoning** **1 teaspoon Spike seasoning** **2 Tablespoons Bragg Liquid Aminos** **1 1/2 cups water** until well mixed Cook over medium heat until thick and glazed

Lentil Burgers Diane

A High-Protein BURGER.

Cook	**1/2 cup lentils** **1 1/2 cups water** **1 teaspoon sea salt,** cook for 30-40 minutes. Drain
Melt	**3 Tablespoons butter**
Add	**1 cup chopped onions** **2 cloves minced garlic** **1 teaspoon vege- sal** **1 Tablespoon Bragg Liquid Aminos.** Remove from heat
Add	lentils to **3/4 cup whole wheat bread crumbs** **1/4 cup wheat germ** **1/2 cup grated carrots** **1/2 cup chopped walnuts** **2 eggs**
Mix	with onion mixture. Form into patties and sauté until brown
Top	burgers with sliced mushrooms, sautéed in **butter and**

Bragg Liquid Aminos. Sprinkle with minced **parsley**.

Soy Burgers

Soak soy beans in cold water overnight. Cook one cup soy beans to three cups water approximately one and a half hours or until tender. Save soy water for gravy.

Sauté   **2 Tablespoons Oil**
                2 Tablespoons chopped green onions

Mix into   **1 cup cooked mashed soy beans**
                1 cup cooked brown rice
                1/2 cup grated Jack cheese
                1 cup ground sunflower seeds
                1/3 cup whole wheat flour
                2 lightly beaten eggs
                1 teaspoon vege-sal
                3 Tablespoons Bragg Liquid Aminos
                1/2 teaspoon basil, shape into patties

Grill   on lightly oiled griddle. Can also be baked in 350° oven for 20 minutes.
Sprinkle with **toasted sesame seeds**

Serve   on a **whole wheat bun or with Soy Gravy**

Soy Gravy

Toast   **1/4 cup whole wheat flour** in dry pan
on medium heat. Remove from pan.

Sauté in   **1/4 cup oil**
                1 chopped onion

Stir   in flour and cook for a few minutes

Add   **2 cups soy water** (from cooking soy beans)
                1 teaspoon vege-sal
                1/2 teaspoon marjoram
                Dash of garlic powder
                Dash of cayenne pepper. Simmer 10 minutes

Broccoli Supreme

A broccoli, cheese, rice casserole with green chilies. Try it, you'll like it!

Sauté in	**2-3 Tablespoons soy oil** **1 medium onion,** chopped **2 large garlic,** chopped until soft
Add	**2 cups peeled chopped broccoli,** cook till bright green
Beat	**4 large eggs** in a large bowl
Add	broccoli mixture to **1 1/2 cup milk** **2 cups cooked brown rice** **1 1/2 cup coarsely grated sharp cheddar** or **jack cheese** **One 4 oz. can chopped drained green chilies** **1 Tablespoon Bragg Liquid Aminos** **1 teaspoon vege-sal**
Pour	into a 2 quart baking dish
Bake	at 350° for 35-40 minutes
Stand	10 minutes before serving

Mushroom Broccoli

Sunday Brunch will be made "special" with this delicious recipe.

CREPE RECIPE

Put	in blender **1 cup unbleached flour** **1 cup milk** **2 eggs** **Dash of vege-sal**
Blend	well. Fry crepes in a pan, layer between paper towels

140

Mushroom Broccoli Filling

Melt	in medium pan **4 Tablespoons butter**
Add	**2 Tablespoons chopped onion**, cooked till glazed
Add	**2 cups sliced, peeled broccoli** in round slices Cook until bright green
Add	**2 cups sliced fresh mushrooms** **2 Tablespoons fresh lemon or lime juice** Cook until mushrooms are glazed
Add	**1 teaspoon vege-sal** **1 teaspoon Bragg Liquid Aminos** **Dash of cayenne pepper** **Pinch of grated nutmeg**
Add	**2 Tablespoons unbleached flour** **2 cups milk.** Stir and cook till thick and creamy

Sherry Cheese Sauce

Melt	in a saucepan **4 Tablespoons butter**
Add	**4 Tablespoons unbleached flour.** Stir
Add	**2 cups milk.** Cook till it thickens
Add	**1 Tablespoon Sherry** **1/4 cup grated mild cheddar cheese.** Keep warm!
Fill	crepe with 2 Tablespoons **Mushroom Broccoli filling.** Fold in thirds. Place on serving dish or individual plates
Top	with **2 Tablespoons Sherry Cheese sauce** Garnish with minced **parsley**

Pasta Melazane

A wonderful "pot luck" casserole. Spaghetti squash may be substituted for the noodles for an all vegetable dish.

Steam	until tender **2-3 medium size eggplant**, sliced in 1/2 rounds
Boil	**8 ozs. Vegeroni ribbon noodles** 8-10 minutes in 1 Tablespoon oil and sea salt Drain and rinse in cold water. DO NOT OVERCOOK
Sauté	**4 minced garlic** in oil with **1 Medium sliced onion** till glazed
Add	**1 small jar of spaghetti sauce** with **1 cup water** **10 fresh basil leaves** chopped **OR** **1/2 teaspoon dry basil** **1 teaspoon vege-sal** **Dash of cayenne pepper** (fresh tomatoes may be blended and added to the sauce)
Sprinkle	oiled 9 x 11 pan with **1/4 cup whole wheat breadcrumbs**
Place	a layer of noodles in bottom of pan
Add	sauce, layer of eggplant, **sliced jack cheese**
Continue	layering finishing with a layer of cheese
Sprinkle	**1/4 cup whole wheat breadcrumbs** over cheese
Bake	at 350° for 20-30 minutes

Zucchini Lasagna

You will not miss the pasta in this tasty "lasagna" dish.

Slice thin	**3 large zucchini** lengthwise 1.4 inch thick Cook till limp in large pan lightly salted water or Covered, steam for 3
Cook	**4 cups spaghetti sauce** or use prepared sauce
Spoon	thin layer of sauce in bottom of oblong casserole dish
Sprinkle	**1/2 cup whole wheat breadcrumbs** over sauce Add layer of zucchini, fitting closely together
Combine	**2 lbs. cottage cheese** with **4 eggs**, slightly beaten **2 Tablespoons chopped parsley** **1/2 teaspoon oregano** **1/2 teaspoon sweet basil** **1/2 teaspoon vege-sal** **1/2 cup parmesan cheese** **1 /2 cup whole wheat bread crumbs** **Dash of cayenne**
Spoon	1 /2 of combined cottage cheese mixture over zucchini
Sprinkle	with grated **mozzarella cheese**
Spoon	sauce over cheese. Repeat layers
Bake	at 350° for 1 hour
Cool	slightly before slicing

Pasta Primavera

A wonderful and tasty pasta dish

Boil	**1 lb. spaghetti** in **1 Tablespoon oil** **1 teaspoon sea salt**, keep hot
Sauté	in order in **1/4 cup water** **2 Tablespoons butter** **2 zucchini cut in 1 inch squares** **2 cups broccoli flowerets** **3 cloves minced garlic** **1 bunch green onions** in 1 1/2 inch lengths **1 bunch asparagus** cut into 1 inch lengths (diagonal) **1 red bell pepper** cut in strips **1 teaspoon vege-sal** **2-3 Tablespoons Bragg Liquid Aminos** Cook for 3-5 minutes
Toss	vegetable mixture into hot spaghetti
Sprinkle	with **fresh grated parmesan cheese.** Serve at once

Spinach Cheese Squares

An excellent luncheon dish. "Popeye" would have loved this

Sauté	**1 medium chopped onion** **3 garlic cloves**, minced **1 teaspoon vege-sal** **1 Tablespoon Bragg Liquid Aminos** Cook until glazed
Chop	**1 1/2 -2 bunches fresh spinach OR** **2 boxes THAWED and DRAINED** **Chopped spinach**

Mix with	**1/2 cup whole wheat flour** **Dash of cayenne pepper** **6 eggs well beaten** **2 cups low fat cottage cheese** **4 cups grated sharp cheddar cheese**, tightly packed Mix all ingredients well and spread into oiled 11 x 7 inch casserole
Bake	in 350° oven for 30-40 minutes or until set Cut into squares

Laurie's Green Fettuccini

A delightful change from the traditional Alfredo

Heat	in Wok **2 Tablespoons oil** **4 Tablespoons butter**
Add	and sauté **2 cups sliced, peeled broccoli** in rounds till bright green
Add	**1 cup sliced green onion**, bulb ends **2 cloves mince garlic** **1 teaspoon basil** **1 teaspoon vege-sal** **1 Tablespoon Bragg Liquid Aminos**
Add	**8 oz. cooked fettuccini noodles or** **Vegeroni noodles.** Keep hot
Cream	in blender **2 cups cottage cheese** with **1/2 cup chicken broth** or **2% milk** **1/4 cup chopped parsley** Add to noodle mixture. Heat thoroughly
Stir in	**1 cup freshly grated parmesan cheese** **1/4 cup grated Swiss cheese** till melted in noodle-cheese mixture. Blend well
Sprinkle	with **minced parsley**

Spaghetti with Meatless Meatballs

The meatballs take a lot of time to make but it is well worth the effort

Mix	together thoroughly **1/2 cup grated cheese** **1/2 cup chopped walnuts** **1 cup whole wheat bread crumbs** **1/2 cup onion,** chopped fine **1 clove minced garlic** **1 Tablespoon chopped parsley** **1 teaspoon sage** **1 teaspoon vege-sal** **1 teaspoon beef seasoning** **1 Tablespoon Bragg Liquid Aminos** Form into small 1 inch balls by squeezing in hand
Sauté	in a little oil until brown on all sides
Place	"meatballs" on spaghetti. Pour hot sauce over pasta
	SAUCE
Sauté in	**2 Tablespoons safflower oil** **1 chopped onion** **2 cloves garlic,** minced **2 stalks sliced celery** **1/2 bell pepper,** chopped
Add	**1 cup chopped fresh mushrooms**
Add	**3 cups meatless spaghetti sauce** **2 large tomatoes** blended in a blender OR **1 large can tomato puree** **15 oz. can tomato sauce** **1/2 teaspoon vege-sal**
Add	**1 teaspoon oregano** **1 small bunch of fresh basil,** chopped
Simmer	for 30 minutes and serve on **whole wheat spaghetti**

146

Noodles Romanoff

This simple, prepare-ahead casserole dish is perfect for an intimate dinner for two or for a party buffet. Serve with crusty French bread and a green salad. Brace yourself for a score of compliments!

Sauté	**1 medium chopped onion** with **4 minced garlic cloves** in a little oil
Add	**1 teaspoon of salt** **1 teaspoon of pepper** **1/2 teaspoon sugar** **15 oz. can tomato sauce**
Simmer	30 minutes
Mix	**3 oz. package softened cream cheese** **1 carton of light sour cream** **6 scallions (green onions)** minced
Boil	**1/2 package Vegeroni ribbon noodles or spinach noodles** for 5 minutes (better undercooked)
Spray	**vegetable oil** in a medium size casserole. Alternate sauce, cream cheese mixture and noodles in 2 layers
Sprinkle	top with **1/2 -3/4cup grated Monterey jack cheese**
Bake	at 350° for 30 minutes. If recipe is doubled, bake 45 min to 1 hour. **Do not overcook.**

Bean Tostada

These refried beans taste so much better than the canned variety. Very simple to prepare.

Soak	**pinto beans** overnight or In the morning for dinnertime Allow **1/2 cup dry beans** per serving (1 cup dry beans to 2 cups water)

Use	Pressure cooker for 25 minutes or 1 hour to 1 1/2 hours on stove with **2 Tablespoons oil**
Mash	beans with enough **bean liquid** to make a soft mixture
Sauté	**1 small onion** with **2 cloves chopped garlic**, add beans
Add	**1 1/2 teaspoon vege-sal** **3 Tablespoons Bragg Liquid Aminos**
Cover	and keep warm until serving time
Serve	on **tostada shells** topped with **shredded lettuce, chopped tomatoes, chopped onions, shredded cheese and guacamole. OLE!**

Mushroom Chili Enchiladas

Created for the *Living Foods* Kitchen; you'll want to prepare for second helping.

SAUCE

Sauté	**1 large diced onion** in **2 Tablespoons cold pressed oil**, add **3 cloves minced garlic** until glazed
Add	**16 oz. bottle spaghetti sauce** **1 1/2 cups of water** **1 Tablespoon chili powder** **2 Teaspoons oregano** **2 teaspoons honey** **1 teaspoon vege-sal** **1 teaspoon ground cumin** **1 teaspoon ground coriander** **Dash of cayenne pepper**
Bring	to boil and simmer for 10 minutes Cover and keep warm

FILLING

Sauté	**1 1/2 pounds thickly sliced mushrooms** in **4 Tablespoons butter** until glazed and gold
Add	**1 can (7 oz.) diced green chiles** **1 cup sliced green onions** **1 cup unflavored yogurt** **1 small package diced cream cheese** **3 Tablespoons whole wheat flour**
Cook	until mixture thickens. Remove from heat
Have	**10 corn tortillas** ready
Dip	with tongs 1 tortilla at a time in enchilada sauce to soften Place in 9 x 13 inch dish
Spoon	about 1/2 cup mushroom sauce in center of tortilla and roll to enclose placing seam side down
Pour	remaining sauce over enchiladas
Cover	with foil and bake at 375° for 20 minutes
Sprinkle	**1 1/2 cups grated Monterey jack cheese** over top
Cook	uncovered for about 5 minutes until cheese is melted

Green Chili Quiche

A real man's quiche! Guaranteed to please! You would "walk a mile" for this one.

Place	**a large corn or whole wheat tortilla** on the bottom of a 9 inch pie pan
Sauté in	**1 Tablespoon butter** **1/2 cup thinly sliced onions** **4 oz. can chopped green chiles**, drained
Spread	onion, chili mixture on the corn tortillas

Add	**2 cups of grated Monterey jack cheese**
Blend	in a blender **4 eggs** **1 cup cottage cheese** **1/2 cup milk** **1 teaspoon vege-sal**
Pour	over cheese
Bake	at 350° for 30-35 minutes Set 10 minutes before serving

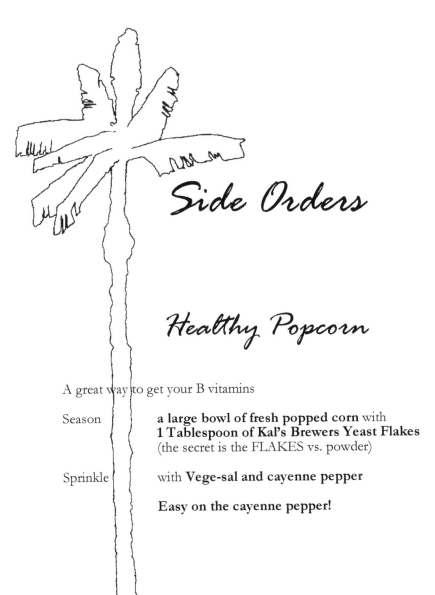

Side Orders

Healthy Popcorn

A great way to get your B vitamins

Season **a large bowl of fresh popped corn** with
1 Tablespoon of Kal's Brewers Yeast Flakes
(the secret is the FLAKES vs. powder)

Sprinkle with **Vege-sal and cayenne pepper**

Easy on the cayenne pepper!

Broiled Topping for Vegetables

Delicious over **broccoli, fresh asparagus or cauliflower.**

Steam   **above vegetables.** DO NOT OVERCOOK.

Mix   together
1/2 cup light mayonnaise
1/4 cup grated parmesan cheese
2 teaspoons chopped parsley
2 teaspoons lemon juice

Beat   **2 egg whites** until stiff. Fold into mayonnaise mixture
Spoon over vegetables and broil until golden brown

Ono Rice

Ono means "delicious" in Hawaiian. Taste and see!

Boil   **1 cup Adzuki beans** in
2 cups water
1 teaspoon vege-sal for 20-30 minutes

Sauté   **3 Tablespoons soy oil**
3 cloves mined garlic
1 large bell pepper, diced
1/2 large round onion, diced
8-10 green onion stalks in 1/4 inch pieces
In a wok or a large frying pan

Add   **1 Tablespoon Bragg Liquid Aminos**
2 Tablespoons Tamari
1 cup fresh mushrooms, sliced
2 cups broccoli flowerets.
Cook until broccoli is bright green

Add   **2-3 cups cooked brown rice** and **beans**

Stir   until well heated. Serve on platter

Garnish   with **minced parsley, toasted sesame seeds, parmesan cheese**

152

Creamed Onions

Traditional in the Bachran's *Thanksgiving* menu. A must at your holiday feast. Can be made early-heat in the microwave or oven before serving.

Peel   **15-20 medium boiler onions**

Place   in medium saucepan and cover with water
Bring to a boil, discard water (this step takes away the onion smell) refill pan with fresh water. Bring to a Boil, lower the temperature and simmer until tender Approximately 30 minutes.

Drain   in a colander

Melt   **4 Tablespoons butter** in saucepan

Put   **4 Tablespoons whole wheat flour**
1 1/2 cup milk
1 teaspoon vege-sal
Dash of cayenne pepper
Blend in blender

Stir   flour mixture into butter and cook stirring until Sauce thickens

Put   drained onions in small casserole. Add sauce

Sprinkle **chopped parsley** over onions.

Holiday Yams

Flavored with orange juice, these yams will compliment your holiday feasts! This dish can also be made ahead and popped in the oven before serving

Bake   **4-6 large garnet red yams**
In 350° oven for 30-45 minutes, until soft. Cool. Peel and quarter

Put   yams through a ricer or mash well

Put	in a casserole dish
Dot	with **2 Tablespoons softened butter** **Juice of 1 large orange** **1 teaspoon cinnamon**
Top	with **large marshmallows**
Bake	at 350° until marshmallows are golden brown and yams are hot. Serve

Potatoes Zucchini Casserole

Delicious blend of ingredients, serve with **salad and French bread**

Sauté	**2 medium or 1 large thinly sliced onion** in **2 Tablespoons safflower oil** with **2 large cloves minced garlic** **1/2 teaspoon each basil, oregano, thyme**
Slice	**1 large or 2 medium potatoes** (leave skin) Arrange on bottom of oiled casserole Spread glazed onion mixture over potato layer
Dribble	**1/3 cup buttermilk** over onions and potatoes
Slice	**1 large zucchini** into 1/4 inch slices and arrange over onions
Sprinkle	mixture of 1/2 teaspoon each; basil, oregano, thyme, Vege-sal and dash of cayenne pepper over zucchini
Spread	**1 1/2 cups grated cheddar cheese** over zucchini slices Cover with foil
Bake	at 350° for 35-40 minutes. DO NOT OVERBAKE

Green Chili Potatoes

A delightful zesty dish. Easy to prepare. A perfect addition to any meal

Grate	**3-4 large potatoes.** Put in ice water
Mix	**8 oz. container light sour cream** **4 Tablespoons milk**
Place	1/2 of drained potatoes in an oiled 9 x 13 inch baking casserole Spread 1/2 of the sour cream mixture over the potatoes
Sprinkle	lightly with **vege-sal, garlic salt, fresh ground pepper**
Spread	**1/2 can diced green chiles** **1/2 of one round onion**, chopped **1/2 cup grated Monterey jack cheese**
Repeat	layers of potatoes, sour cream, seasonings, chili, onions, and cheese. Bake at 350° for 35-40 minutes

Chin Lam's
Super Bean Casserole

Delicious with a large green salad and crusty French bread!

Sauté	**8 slices of low fat bacon**, cut into squares until light brown
Add	**2 chopped medium onions.** Cook until transparent
Mix	together in a large casserole Bacon and onion mixture **Two 1 lb. cans of baked beans** **Two 1 lb. cans of kidney beans** **Two 1 lb. cans of baby lima beans**, drained **1/2 lb. monterey jack cheese** cut into small cubes **1 cup light brown sugar** **2/3 cup catsup** **4 teaspoons Worchestershire sauce** Dash of garlic salt
Sprinkle	generously with parmesan cheese. Bake at 350°, 1 hour

Hot Sweet Mustard

Homemade mustard that reminds you of your favorite "deli." Hot enough for you to sit up and take notice!

Blend	in a small bowl **6 Tablespoons dry mustard** **1 Tablespoon flour** **2 Tablespoons sugar** **1 teaspoon salt** **1 teaspoon Worchestershire sauce** **1/4 teaspoon prepared horseradish**
Add	**4 Tablespoons cider vinegar**, one tablespoon at a time, stirring well. Mustard should have the consistency of thick cream. Makes about 1/3 cup Keeps well in refrigerator

Nutty Buddy Sandwich

A favorite with the younger set and the young at heart!

Toast	**2 slices of 9 grain bread**
Spread	**unsalted natural peanut butter** on one slice of bread
Slice	lengthwise 1/4 inch thick **1 banana** and place on top of peanut butter
Spread	layer of **raw honey** on second slice of bread
Sprinkle	**2 teaspoons of raisins** on honey
Put	sandwich together

Mushroom Melt Sandwich

Wonderful crunchy sandwich, good for lunch or a light dinner

Toast	**2 slices of 9 grain bread** And lightly spread with **cold processed mayonnaise**
Slice	**6-8 fresh mushrooms** and place on one toasted bread slice
Place	**2 slices of Monterey jack cheese** or **mozzarella** on mushrooms
Place	under toaster broiler to melt cheese
Put	on other piece of toast **2 slices of tomatoes** **3 slices of Japanese cucumbers** **a small handful of red clover or alfalfa sprouts**
Season	with **vege-sal** **Dash of cayenne pepper**
Put	sandwich together

Tuna Medley Sandwich

Use white Albacore tuna for the best flavor

Mix	**1 can of white Albacore tuna with** **1 Tablespoon of green onions**
Moisten	with **plain yogurt**
Serve	on toasted **9 grain bread** with **tomatoes, cucumbers and red clover** or **alfalfa sprouts**
Season	with **vege-sal and cayenne pepper**

Breads

Living Foods Special Cornbread

Good old fashioned corn bread with good old fashioned flavor. A much requested recipe

Blend	in a large bowl **2 cups yellow corn meal** **1 cup whole wheat flour** **1 cup unbleached flour** **2 Tablespoons baking powder** **1 teaspoon salt** **1/2 cup turbinado sugar** **1/4 cup melted butter**
Blend	in a blender **3 large eggs** **2 cups milk** **1 large orange** peeled, seeded and quartered
Add	wet ingredients to dry
Mix	until just blended
Pour	into 9 x 11 inch pan (greased and floured)
Bake	350° for 35 minutes

French Bread

French bread, made in your own kitchen. You will be pleased with the results. Not only for the brave.

Pour	**2 1/2 cups warm water** into a large mixing bowl
Sprinkle	**3 packages dry active yeast** over the water stirring until dissolved
Add	**1 Tablespoon salt** **1 Tablespoon soft butter**
Beat	in **7 1/2 cups unsifted whole wheat** or **unbleached flour,** gradually. Dough will be sticky
Knead	on a lightly floured counter or board until smooth and elastic. Approximately 10 minutes.
Place	dough in a greased bowl
Brush	top of dough with **safflower oil** and COVER Let it rise in a warm place, free from drafts until double in bulk. (1 hour)
Punch	down and let it rise again for 15 minutes
Divide	dough into three parts
Roll	each piece on a floured counter into a rectangle Beginning at the wide end, roll dough tightly towards you
Place	roll seam side down on a baking sheet 4 inches apart
Cut	with scissors, 4 diagonal gashes on top of each loaf
Brush	top of each loaf with warm water and **sprinkle with cornmeal.** Let it rise until doubled, about 30 minutes
Bake	in a hot oven 425° about 30 minutes until crisp and brown

Puri

Try this simple Indian bread recipe developed at the Kamehameha Schools by Olga Sand for the International Food Classes.

Mix	**4 cups unbleached flour,** unsifted **1/4 teaspoon salt** **1/4 teaspoon baking powder** **1/4 teaspoon sugar** in a large mixing bowl
Add	**4 1/2 Tablespoons shortening** and rub with fingers until mixture is crumbly
Pour	in **1/2 cup water** and knead to make a soft dough. Continue kneading for about 10 minutes adding **1/4 cup water** as needed. (dough should be firm, like stiff yeast dough)
Make	a depression in top of dough and spoon in **1 Tablespoon water**
Cover	with dampened cloth and let rest for 30 minutes
Pinch	off small balls the size of a large walnut and roll out on lightly floured surface into 5 inch rounds 1/16 to 1/32 inch thick
Drop	rounds, one at a time, into **hot oil 1 inch deep**. Tap top of round as you drop it into the hot fat. When the dough puffs up and is brown underneath, turn over and brown other side. Serve hot. Makes 24 large PURI

Chapatis

Mix	1/2 lb. white and whole wheat flour (half and half) Add a pinch of salt to the flour mixture
Cut	or rub in 1 oz. butter until mixture is crumbly
Make	into a soft dough with cold water, adding water gradually. Cover with damp cloth; let rest for 1 hour
Knead	well. Divide into billiard ball size and roll to saucer size
Bake	on a greased griddle using low heat

Desserts

Apple Walnut Raisin Rice Pudding

Delicious with honey-sweetened yogurt

Combine   together
                 2 cups cooked brown rice
                 3 cups milk
                 3 large beaten eggs
                 3 tablespoons raw honey
                 1 cup golden raisins
                 1 grated green apple
                 1/2 cup chopped walnuts
                 1 teaspoon cinnamon
                 1 teaspoon grated orange rind
                 1/4 teaspoon nutmeg
                 1 Tablespoon whole wheat flour

Pour   into oiled casserole dish

Bake   350° for 30 minutes

Cottage Nut Bars

Mini cheesecake squares

Combine	**1 cup whole wheat flour** **1 block butter** **3 Tablespoons turbinado sugar**
Press	in 8 x 8 inch pan
Bake	at 350° for 15 minutes
Blend	**1 egg** **3 oz. light cream cheese** **1/3 cup cottage cheese** **3 Tablespoons raw honey** **1 Tablespoon vanilla extract**
Pour	over the baked crust. Sprinkle with **1/2 cup chopped pecans**
Bake	at 350° for 15-20 minutes

Cottage Cheese Pie

A wonderful substitute for cheesecake – smooth, creamy and not too sweet

Crush	**1/2 package chocolate or vanilla health cookies**
Mix with	**2 teaspoons cinnamon** **1/3 cup butter**
Press	into a quiche pan Bake at 350° for 10 minutes, cool
Blend	in blender **2 Tablespoons cold water** **2 Tablespoons lemon juice** **5 Tablespoons agar flakes** **1/3 cup honey plus 1 Tablespoon** **Yolks of 2 large eggs**

Add	**2 cups cottage cheese** **1 Tablespoon vanilla**
Pour	into pie shell
Chill	overnight. Serve with **sliced, fresh strawberries**.

Oatmeal Cake

This is in the "must try" category. Simply scrumptious!

Pour	**1 1/2 cups boiling water over** **1 cup quick cooking oats**. Mix well. Set aside.
Cream	**1/2 cup butter** **1 cup brown sugar**, firmly packed **1 cup sugar**, thoroughly
Beat	in **2 eggs**; stir in soaked oatmeal
Sift	together **1 1/2 cups flour** **1 teaspoon baking soda** **1 teaspoon nutmeg** **1 teaspoon cinnamon** **1/2 teaspoon salt**
Stir	into oatmeal mixture
Turn	into greased 13 x 9 x 2 inch pan
Bake	at 350° for 30-35 minutes
Cool	in pan; spread with the following topping

Broiled Topping

Mix	in a small bowl
	1/4 cup brown sugar
	1/2 cup sugar
	1 cup flaked coconut
	1 cup chopped nuts
	6 tablespoons butter
	1/4 cup light cream
	1/4 teaspoon vanilla extract
	Dribble over oatmeal cake
Broil	until golden (about 5 minutes)

Hawaiian Orange Nut Cake

A moist cake - perfect for picnics.

Squeeze	**juice from one large orange.** Set aside.
Grind	together in meat grinder or food processor
	seeded orange pulp and rind
	1 cup raisins
Add	**1/3 cup unsalted macadamia nuts**, finely chopped
Mix	in a large bowl
	2 cups whole wheat flour
	1 teaspoon baking soda
	1/2 teaspoon salt
	1 cup sugar
Add	**1/2 cup softened butter**
	1 cup milk
	2 eggs, unbeaten
	Beat at low speed 2 minutes; at high speed 2 minutes
Fold	orange, nuts and raisin mixture into batter
	Pour into well-greased 9 x 13 inch pan
Bake	at 350° for 40-50 minutes

Orange Butter Nut Frosting

Prick	cake with fork
Drip	**1/3 to1/2 cup orange juice** over warm cake
Combine	**1/3 cup sugar** **1 teaspoon cinnamon** **1/4 teaspoon nutmeg** **1/4 cup chopped macadamia nuts**
Sprinkle	over cake

German Apple Butter Cake

Fresh sliced green apples and fresh orange juice gives this butter cake a special flavor. Yummy!

Whip	at high speed in large mixer **2 blocks butter** **1/2 cup sugar** until light and creamy
Add	**2 large eggs**, one at a time. Beat well.
Alternate	**1/2 cup fresh orange juice**, with **2 cups unbleached flour**, sifted with **1 teaspoon baking powder** Spread onto a 7 x 11 inch greased and floured pan
Core	peel and quarter **3 large green apples** Cut each quarter into 3 wedges
Stick	wedges, sharp edge down into batter in long rows
Sprinkle	top of cake with **1 teaspoon cinnamon** mixed with **1/2 cup sugar**
Bake	at 350° for 45 minutes

Honey Carrot Cake

A wonderful blend of flavors. Can be made into muffins for the lunch box

Combine	**2 cups whole wheat flour** **2 teaspoons baking soda** **3 teaspoons cinnamon** **1/4 teaspoon nutmeg** **1 teaspoon salt** **1/4 cup wheat germ**
Beat	together **2 cups honey** **1 cup safflower oil** **4 large eggs**
Add	to dry ingredients
Fold In	**3 cups grated carrots** **1 cup crushed pineapple** **1/2 cup chopped pecans**
Pour	into a 9 x 13 inch pan
Bake	at 350° for 40-45 minutes

Zucchini Deluxe Cake

Delicious and moist with carob chips for added nutrition

Cream	together **1 block butter** **1/2 cup cold processed oil** **1 1/4 cup turbinado sugar**
Beat	**2 eggs** **1 teaspoon vanilla** **1/2 cup buttermilk**
Add	to butter mixture. Mix well

Add	2 1/2 cups unbleached flour
	1 teaspoon baking soda
	1/2 teaspoon baking powder
	1/2 teaspoon cinnamon
	1/2 teaspoon ground cloves
	1/4 teaspoon salt

Fold in	2 cups finely diced zucchini (1 large)
	DO NOT GRATE
	1 cup carob chips

Pour	into oiled, floured or waxed paper-lined 9 x 13 inch pan

Bake	at 325° 40-45 minutes

Kulolo

Ono (delicious) steamed Hawaiian Coconut Pudding!

Grate	very fine
	1 cup peeled, uncooked taro

Add	1/2 cup coconut milk (frozen)
	1/2 cup dark brown sugar
	1/2 cup finely grated fresh coconut

Line	aluminum pie pan that has a *puka bottom with ti leaves or foil

Pour	taro mixture into pan

Steam	over water in covered pot for 1 hour

holes.

Cooking Methods

Baste: To moisten meat during cooking by pouring small amounts of juice or marinade over the meat.

Boil: Liquid or sauce will bubble constantly while cooking on a medium-high heat.

Broil: To cook under high, direct heat, usually in the oven.

Cut in: Blending in cold shortening with a wire blender or two knives into the flour.

Deep fry: To use hot oil to completely cover food

Dot: To distribute butter or herbs over the surface of the food.

Fold: To mix ingredients with a gentle over and over motion.

Knead: To work dough by lifting and pressing and pressing down with the palms of your hands.

Marinate: Allowing meat to stand in sauce mixture for seasoning.

Mince: To chop or cut very fine.

Parboil: To partially cook meat or vegetables in water or soup stock.

Pare: To remove outer skin or rind.

Poach: To cook briefly in hot liquid just below the boiling point.

Sauté: To fry in a small amount of fat.

Scald: To bring milk just to the boiling point.

Shred: To cut, slice or tear into narrow strips.

Steam: Place in a tightly covered pot of boiling water, allowing the steam to cook the food for a given length of time.

Table of Equivalents

3 teaspoons = 1 tablespoon

2 Tablespoons = 1 ounce

4 Tablespoons = 2 ounces or 1/4 cup

8 Tablespoons = 4 ounces or 1/2 cup

2 cups = 1 pint

4 cups = 1 quart

1/2 cup butter = 1 block butter or 1/4 lb.

1 cup butter = 2 blocks butter or 1/2 lb.

2 cups butter = 4 blocks butter or 1 lb.

1 Tablespoon cornstarch = 2 Tablespoons flour.

1 square unsweetened chocolate = 3 Tablespoons cocoa + 2 teaspoons shortening.

1 cup sour milk = 1 Tablespoon vinegar + sweet milk to fill 1 cup.

1 cup sweet milk =1/2 cup evaporated milk + 1/2 cup water.

1 cup pastry flour = 1 cup + 2 Tablespoons sifted cake flour.

Shoyu = soy sauce

*All measurements are level unless otherwise indicated.

*Certain brands of shoyu are more strongly flavored than others.
If the one you are using seems salty, adjust the marinating time down
and adjust the flavor by adding more broth or liquid to the gravy stock.

*Always bake on the racks in the center of the oven, usually the rack
second from the bottom of the oven.

Notes

Notes

Notes

Notes

Notes

Made in the USA
Lexington, KY
05 June 2015